Seafood
Twice a Week

Design, Erica Ridout
Illustrations, Karen Simms
Production, Technigraphic Systems, Inc.
Editor, Sandy Mael
Cover photo, Alaska Seafood Marketing Institute

Published by National Seafood Educators
Printed in the United States of America

Seafood
Twice a Week

Evie Hansen and Cindy Welke Snyder, RD, MPH

National Seafood Educators
Richmond Beach, Washington

Inquiries should be addressed to:

Permissions Department
National Seafood Educators
P.O. Box 60006
Richmond Beach, WA 98177
(206) 546-6410 Fax: (206) 546-6411
email: msn.eviense

Printed and bound in the United States of America
First Edition
March, 1997
Second Printing
December, 1997

ISBN: 0-9616426-4-5
Library of Congress Catalog Card Number: 95-70435-1997

Publisher's Cataloging in Publication
Hansen, Evie.
    Seafood twice a week / Evie Hansen and Cindy Welke Snyder.
    p. cm
    Includes bibliographical references and index.
    Preassigned LCCN: 95-70435
    ISBN 0-9616426-4-5

    1. Seafood. 2. Cookery (Seafood) 3. Health-Nutritional aspects. I. Snyder, Cindy Welke. II. Title.

TX747.H36 1997   641.6'92
                         QBJ97-40214

To the Creator of the sea, rivers and lakes
which are on loan to us for the care of their bounty.

Table of Contents

CHAPTER 1: Nutrition

Seafood 3
The Health Food from the Sea 3
Why *Seafood Twice a Week?* 5
The Unique Benefits of Seafood 7
A Historical Perspective 8
Omega-3's and Heart Disease 9
Omega 3's and Cancer 10
Diabetes 11
Other Health Benefits 13
Are Omega-3 Fatty Acids Essential
    for Good Health? 14
Is Shellfish Heart-Healthy? 15
Nutritional Comparisons 17

CHAPTER 2: Safety

How Safe is Seafood? 21
Facts About Seafood Safety 21
Consider Safety First...
    Buy From a Reputable Source 23
If You Are the Source of Your Seafood 24
Consider Safety First...
    Avoid Eating Raw Seafood 25
Consider Safety First...
    When Handling Seafood in Your Home 28
Concerns for Sulfite-Sensitive Individuals 31
Sulfites 31
Sources of Additional Safety Information 32

CHAPTER 3: Preparation

How to Evaluate a Seafood Counter 35
   How to Pick Out the Best
   and Keep it That Way .36

How to Substitute Seafood 39

Keeping Seafood Safe at Home 40
   Bringing Seafood Home 40
   Storing Fresh Seafood 40
   Thawing Frozen Seafood 42
   Refreezing Seafood 42
   All Shapes and Sizes 43
     Drawn 43
     Fillets 43
     Dressed 43
     Steaks 43
     How to Fillet a Round-Bodied Fish 44
     How to Steak a Salmon .44
     How to Fillet a Flat Fish 44
     How to Open a Clam 45
     How to Shuck an Oyster 45
     How to Clean a Mussel .45
     How to Dress a Soft-Shell Crab 46
     How to Crack a Crab 46
     How to Clean a Shrimp .46
     How to Dress a Lobster .47
     How To Dress a Squid 47

How to Cook Heart Smart 48
   10-Minute-Per-Inch Rule for Fish 48
   Moist Heat Cooking Techniques 49
   Dry Heat Cooking Techniques 51

Ready to Eat Processed Seafood 53
   Smoked Seafood 53

Landing a Seafood Bargain 55

CHAPTER 4: Appetizers 57

Table of Contents

CHAPTER 5: Soups & Stews 73

CHAPTER 6: Sandwiches 85

CHAPTER 7: Salads 99

CHAPTER 8: Finfish Entrées 113

CHAPTER 9: Shellfish Entrées 139

CHAPTER 10: Microwave 161

CHAPTER 11: Grilling 179

CHAPTER 12: Special Events 195

CHAPTER 13: Recreational Fishing
Concerns for the Recreational
or Subsistence Angler 211
Bacterial and Viral Infection 212
Concerns for Medically
"High Risk" Individuals 213
Parasitic Infection 214
Naturally-Occurring Poisons 215
    Ciguatera 215
Paralytic Shellfish Poisoning 216
Scombroid Poisoning 217
Environmental Contaminants 218
    Mercury 218
Polychlorinated Biphenyls (PCBs) 219
Tips for Reducing Your Potential Intake of PCBs .. 220

Selected Bibliography *221*
Index by Title *223*
Index *227*
Ordering Information *235*

Nutrition

1

Nutrition

Seafood

The Health Food from the Sea

Seafood is the perfect choice for health-conscious individuals. The recipes in *Seafood Twice a Week* will provide an excellent source of protein which is also very low in calories, fat, and cholesterol. Two servings of seafood a week is the best way to get omega-3 fatty acids which are beneficial to health.

Seafood is:
- **An excellent source of protein**
- **Low in calories**
- **Low in total fat, saturated fat, and cholesterol**
- **High in polyunsaturated fat**
- **The most significant source of omega-3 fatty acids**
- **Low in sodium**
- **A great source of vitamins and minerals**

Not only is seafood healthful, but it is also convenient to prepare. And with the number of different species available in the marketplace, seafood offers an almost endless variety from which to choose. Seafood twice a week never gets boring!

Seafood is an excellent source of protein.

An average 3¹/₂ ounce serving of seafood provides 17-21 grams of complete protein. That's about half the protein the body needs each day. And because seafood does not contain a lot of connective tissue, it is more easily chewed and digested than most other protein choices.

Seafood is low in calories.

Seafood is the best protein investment for the calorie-conscious consumer. Most seafood contains less than 100 calories in a 3¹/₂ ounce serving. Compare that with 160 calories for a similar portion of chicken and more than 200 calories for beef. A 3¹/₂ ounce fillet of sole will fill half of your plate, giving the appearance of volume—for only 90 calories. And because seafood is so rich in flavor, it does not require much fat and oil to prepare a delicious meal.

Seafood is very low in total fat, saturated fat, and cholesterol.
Many species of seafood have less than one gram of fat per $3^{1}/_{2}$ ounce serving. Health experts recommend that Americans should limit total fat intake to 30% of total calories each day. Most seafood gets 10-30% of its calories from fat. Cholesterol levels are also low in most seafood, with an average of 15-20 mg of cholesterol per ounce compared to 25 mg per ounce for chicken and 30 mg per ounce for beef.

Seafood is high in polyunsaturated fat.
The fat in seafood is predominantly heart-healthy polyunsaturated fat.

Seafood is the most significant source of omega-3 fatty acids.
Seafood provides a unique polyunsaturated fat called omega-3 fatty acids. These fats may have protective benefits against heart disease, cancer, and inflammatory conditions. Seafood is the most significant source of these unique fatty acids.

Seafood is low in sodium.
Seafood is naturally low in sodium. A $3^{1}/_{2}$ ounce serving of finfish provides less than 100 mg of sodium. Shellfish contains more sodium—between 150-300 mg per ounce. The recipes in *Seafood Twice a Week* will provide many ideas for using all varieties of seafood while keeping sodium levels below 800 mg per serving.

Seafood is an excellent source of vitamins and minerals.
Seafood is a good source of B-vitamins, primarily thiamine, riboflavin, and niacin. All species contain substantial amounts of phosphorus and potassium.

Canned anchovies, jack mackerel, salmon, and sardines provide high levels of calcium if packed with bones. Clams, mussels, and oysters are excellent sources of iron and zinc—both nutrients that can be difficult to get in traditional low-cholesterol diets.

Why *Seafood Twice a Week?*

The early observations of Danish investigators Dyerberg and Bang associated health benefits with the native diets of Greenland Eskimos. The health benefits of the Eskimo diet came as a surprise for most researchers. The Eskimo diet clearly contradicted all the nutrition recommendations of the day. Greenland Eskimos commonly consumed one pound of seal and whale meat daily—a relatively high fat diet! Despite this unusual pattern of eating, Greenland natives experienced less heart disease, cancer, and diabetes.

Fortunately, we don't need to eat a pound of whale and seal meat per day to obtain the unique health benefits of seafood. In the past decade, numerous studies have helped health professionals better understand the amount of seafood necessary to promote good health.

An article published in the *New England Journal of Medicine* in May 1985 identified a 50% reduction in death from coronary heart disease associated with the consumption of seven ounces of seafood per week. The article concluded:

> **The consumption of as little as one to two fish dishes per week may be preventive in relation to heart disease.**

Since the publication of this article, every major health organization—the **American Heart Association,** the **National Cancer Institute,** the **American Medical Association,** and many more—has promoted the same message to eat seafood twice a week. Although the message to promote seafood consumption has been clearly endorsed in the US, the educational effort has been piecemeal. No organization has stepped to the helm to organize and initiate a national education campaign to promote seafood twice a week. Until now!

The publication of *Seafood Twice a Week* officially kicks off a national education program designed to:
1. Promote the consumption of two seafood meals per week, and
2. Teach the public how to purchase, handle, and prepare two seafood meals per week.

During the writing of this book, another research article was published that has added more scientific evidence to this health message. A group of Seattle investigators led by Dr. David Siscovick identified that fish consumption was associated with a 50% reduction in the risk of cardiac arrest. It was discovered that one high-fat fish meal or at least two medium-fat fish meals per week produced this benefit. Seafood research continues to affirm that seafood twice a week is the best choice for good health.

The Unique Benefits of Seafood

Omega-3 Fatty Acids

During the past 25 years, considerable research has been devoted to understanding the health benefits of a specific family of polyunsaturated fats present in fish and fish oils. These oils are commonly known as omega-3 fatty acids.

What are Omega-3 Fatty Acids?

Omega-3 fatty acids are a family of particularly long-chained polyunsaturated fats that share a unique chemical structure. These fats are even more unsaturated than vegetable oil. There are seven members of the omega-3 family. The two most prominent omega-3 fatty acids are eicosapentaenoic acid (EPA) and docosahexaenoic acid (DHA). Nutrition values for omega-3 fatty acids generally represent the sum of EPA and DHA.

Initially, the majority of research focused on EPA; more recent studies have looked at the role of DHA. Investigators are curious about the individual roles of both EPA and DHA. Research is now being designed which will help scientists understand if there are optimal levels of each omega-3 fatty acid or perhaps an ideal ratio of EPA to DHA. Answers to these questions will certainly emerge in the next decade.

How are Omega-3 Fatty Acids Beneficial?

Polyunsaturated fats are incorporated into numerous cells of the body and form potent hormone-like substances called eicosanoids. Eicosanoids are believed to play a significant role in boosting the immune response and reducing risk from atherosclerosis, cancer, inflammatory conditions, and allergic reactions. These hormone-like substances are derived from both vegetable and fish oils.

The eicosanoids derived from fish oils differ chemically from vegetable-based eicosanoids and frequently produce a significantly different effect on the body. Often an eicosanoid formed from fish oils will form a substance that, in fact, opposes the action of a vegetable-based eicosanoid. For example, vegetable oils form the eicosanoid thromboxane in the platelet. Thromboxane helps to promote the formation of clots which may clog a narrowing artery. The omega-3 eicosanoid which forms in the platelets opposes clot formation.

Most of the health benefits of omega-3 fatty acids are mediated by eicosanoids.

A Historical Perspective

- Early research in the 1970s linked omega-3 fatty acids with a very low incidence of heart disease among a group of Greenland Eskimos.
- Studies in the 1980s identified a beneficial relation-ship between omega-3's and a number of other chronic conditions, namely cancer, inflammatory conditions, and autoimmune diseases (such as lupus erythematosus).
- In the past ten years, investigators have begun to understand specifically how these fats operate to produce health benefits at the cellular level.
- The presence of omega-3 fatty acids in the nerve tissues of newborns has been associated with optimal health of these tissues. Studies on newborns have led investigators into a new area of research. In addition to playing a preventive role, omega-3 fatty acids appear to be essential to the normal function-ing of the body.
- It is now understood that omega-3 fatty acids could influence functions in almost every organ system of the body.
- Many scientists in the United States are advocating that the government recognize omega-3 fatty acids as essential to health and establish official recom-mendations for dietary intake.

Omega-3's and Heart Disease

Three major factors influence the development and progression of heart disease. Omega-3 fatty acids produce positive effects on each of these three processes:

Process	Benefits of Omega-3 Fatty Acids
Atherosclerosis Arteries narrow due to fat deposits which accumulate on the inside of the artery wall. This process, called atherosclerosis, is a slow, chronic process which results in reduced blood flow to the heart, brain, and other vital organs.	Omega-3's: • Significantly lower triglycerides (circulating fats in the blood) • Produce inconsistent effects on lowering cholesterol and LDL's (low-density lipoproteins) • *May* reduce the progression of atherosclerosis • *May* slow down the rate at which coronary arteries close following the mechanical opening of the artery (angioplasty)
Clot Formation A clot can form and block narrowed arteries. This clot is developed from a clump of aggregated platelets and associated materials.	Omega-3's: • *May* reduce the "stickiness" of platelets, therefore inhibiting clot formation • *May* cause red blood cells to be more slippery so they are better able to "slide" through closing arteries
Blood Vessel Spasms Decreased blood flow can also be produced by spasms of the muscle surrounding the blood vessels. A spasm causes the blood vessel to constrict, further limiting blood flow.	Omega-3's: • *May* help relax blood vessel walls • *May* slightly decrease blood pressure • *May* help maintain the normal rhythm of the heart

Dr. David Siscovick identified an intake of 5.5 mg of omega-3 fatty acids *per month* associated with a 50% reduction in the risk of cardiac arrest. An intake of 5.5 mg of omega-3 fatty acids per month translates to 1.4 mg of omega-3 fatty acids per week—one high-fat fish meal or at least two medium-fat fish meals per week!

Omega 3's and Cancer

Cancer is the second most common cause of death in the US—second only to heart disease. Cancer is not a single disease. Rather, "cancer" refers to a group of diseases in which body cells multiply and spread uncontrollably. Cancer growth can occur in virtually any part of the body.

The development and growth of cancer progresses through a number of stages.

Stage	Potential Benefits of Omega-3 Fatty Acids
Onset Damage to cellular DNA provides the initiation of tumor cells. If the damage is repaired before the cell multiplies, no tumor will occur.	**Omega-3's:** • *May* help healthy cells resist damage by tumor-producing cells.
Multiplication of cells If the damaged cell reproduces, it duplicates the damage. If unchecked, the multiplying cells can develop into a tumor.	**Omega-3's:** • *May* interfere with tumor growth.
Spread The tumor can then keep growing and invade vulnerable tissues.	**Omega-3's:** • *May* inhibit the spread of the tumor throughout the body.

Most of the research on omega-3 fatty acids and cancer has been done on animal subjects. However, in the past five years human studies have begun to emerge. Although the research is not complete, there is a strong suspicion that omega-3 fatty acids may play a protective role in *each stage* of cancer development.

More research is needed to clarify our understanding of the relationship between omega-3 fatty acids and cancer prevention, but the initial results look very promising!

Diabetes

Researchers are currently investigating the possible role of omega-3 fatty acids in the prevention and control of diabetes. Diabetes is a chronic disease in which the body is either unable to produce insulin or incapable of using insulin effectively. Two very different forms of diabetes occur: insulin-dependent diabetes mellitus (IDDM) and non-insulin dependent diabetes mellitus (NIDDM).

Insulin-dependent diabetes mellitus (IDDM), commonly referred to as Type I or juvenile-onset diabetes, is considered an autoimmune disease. Antibodies are formed which attack the insulin-producing cells of the pancreas, leaving them unable to produce insulin.

In non-insulin dependent diabetes mellitus (NIDDM), commonly known as Type II diabetes, the body is able to produce sufficient insulin but tissue is resistent to insulin activity.

Both forms of diabetes are rare among Greenland Eskimos.

Omega-3 fatty acids may play a role in three stages of diabetes: the onset, the control of symptoms, and the management of complications.

Stage of Diabetes	Potential Benefits of Omega-3 Fatty Acids
Onset of diabetes	• Omega-3 fatty acids may keep the immune system in check, therefore reducing the likelihood that the body will "self-destruct" insulin-producing cells.
Control of symptoms	• A low level of Docosahexaenoic acid (DHA) in the muscle cell is associated with an increased insulin resistance. Therefore, blood sugar control may be influenced by the regular consumption of a diet high in omega-3 fatty acids in individuals with NIDDM. **Note:** *Studies have not demonstrated a consistent influence on blood sugar levels.*
Complications of diabetes	• Omega-3 fatty acids may influence the development and progression of cardiovascular disease, the most common and serious complication of diabetes. • Omega-3 fatty acids may delay the onset of kidney and nerve complications or may control the progression of these diseases.

Other Health Benefits

The influence of omega-3 fatty acids on heart disease has been well studied during the past 25 years. Research is also being conducted which suggests that fish oils may help control immune and inflammatory conditions—both surprisingly less common among Greenland Eskimos. In contrast to heart disease research, the relationship between omega-3 fatty acids and immune or inflammatory conditions is at an earlier stage of investigation. Therefore, the relationship is not as clearly understood. Definitive conclusions cannot be drawn from available data. However, omega-3 fatty acids are suspected to produce health benefits in the following diseases:

Disease	Potential Benefits of Omega-3 Fatty Acids
Asthma	• *May* increase resistance to asthma attacks
Inflammatory Bowel Disease	• *May* limit inflammation of intestinal tissues
Kidney Disease	• *May* slow the progression of kidney disease
Lupus Erythematosus	• *May* control immune disease and conditions causing inflammation, rashes, etc.
Migraine Headaches	• *May* interfere with the onset of headaches due to blood vessel dilation
Multiple Sclerosis	• *May* reduce the degree of disability • *May* reduce the frequency, duration, and severity of relapses
Psoriasis	• *May* reduce itching, redness, and scaling
Rheumatoid Arthritis	• Reduce inflammation • Decrease morning stiffness • Decrease joint pain and tenderness

Are Omega-3 Fatty Acids Essential for Good Health?

Omega-3's and Pregnancy

It is now clear that omega-3 fatty acids are essential in early human development. During pregnancy the fetal brain, nervous system, and eye tissues accumulate Docosahexaenoic acid (DHA), one of the omega-3 fatty acids.

This accumulation is most dramatic during the last trimester when DHA concentrations increase three to five times. Animal studies suggest that a deficiency of DHA may result in offspring with irreversible vision problems. Early evidence also suggests that low levels of DHA may be associated with reduced mental ability.

DHA levels are dependent upon the mother's diet during pregnancy.

Requirements for omega-3 fatty acids in pregnancy have not been established. However, a pregnant woman can provide her developing baby with significant DHA by consuming seafood twice a week.

Omega-3 Fatty Acids and the Premature Infant
- Infants born before 32 weeks' gestation have lower body supplies of DHA.
- These infants can "catch up" if they are fed breast milk or a formula supplemented with DHA.

Omega-3 Fatty Acids and the Newborn
- During the first three months of life, DHA concentrations increase three to five times.
- DHA accumulation in the brain continues through the first two years of life.
- **Human milk is the only infant food that provides significant and available forms of omega-3 fatty**

acids. In countries where infant formulas are supplemented with omega-3 fatty acids, DHA is added to duplicate the fatty acid levels of human breast milk. **The DHA content of breast milk is greatly influenced by the mother's diet.** Women who consume seafood have more DHA in their breast milk. Therefore, nursing women should be encouraged to consume seafood twice a week in order to provide an adequate source of DHA.

Omega-3 Fatty Acids Throughout the Lifecycle

Numerous studies suggest that omega-3 fatty acids may be essential throughout the human life cycle. The scientific community has made the following recommendations.

Omega-3 Fatty Acid Recommendation

The adult daily requirement for omega-3 fatty acids is estimated to be 300-400 mg per day (.3 gm-.4 gm daily).

The United States Government and the World Health Organization are being encouraged by prominent scientists worldwide to formally adopt these recommendations.

Is Shellfish Heart-Healthy?

We all know that seafood twice a week is good for us. But does that include shellfish, too? The answer is an emphatic "Yes!"

For many years it was believed that all shellfish were high in cholesterol. As technology has improved, we've learned that this is not the case. Cholesterol belongs to a family of compounds known as sterols which share some chemical features. However, included in the sterol family are a number of non-cholesterol sterols. Early values did not distinguish cholesterol from these non-cholesterol sterols. With more sensitive technology, our current cholesterol values are more accurate. In addition, we now understand that non-cholesterol sterols interfere with absorption of cholesterol, allowing it to pass right through the body.

To fully understand the cholesterol picture, it is important to know that there are two kinds of shellfish: mollusks and crustaceans. Mollusks include clams, mussels, oysters, scallops, and squid. Crustaceans include crab, lobster, and shrimp. The cholesterol content of each group is dependent upon what they eat.

Mollusks are the vegetarians of the sea; they eat tiny sea plants. Because of their low-cholesterol diet, mollusks have less cholesterol, ounce for ounce, than any protein source! Most mollusks provide an average of 30-50 mg of cholesterol per 3$\frac{1}{2}$ ounce serving. However, squid is a notable exception, providing 235 mg cholesterol in the same portion.

As a general rule, crustacean shellfish are higher in cholesterol. Crustaceans are carnivores which feed on small sea animals in addition to plants. Because they consume more cholesterol, they contain more cholesterol (55-150 mg per 3$\frac{1}{2}$ ounce serving).

Many health-conscious individuals have unnecessarily limited their consumption of shrimp because it has 150 mg of cholesterol per serving. An article published in 1990 by Dr. Marian Childs and colleagues at the University of Washington offers good news for shellfish lovers! These researchers identified men who consumed two daily servings of squid or shrimp for a three-week period had no increase in cholesterol or triglycerides.

Nutritional Comparisons

All values per 3 1/2 oz. (100 gm) raw edible portion	Calories	Protein (gms)	Total Fat (gms)	Omega-3 (gms)	Saturated Fat (gms)	Cholesterol (mg)	Sodium (mg)
Finfish							
Anchovy	130	20	5	1.5	1	N/A	105
Bass	115	19	4	0.6	1	70	70
Bass, Striped	95	18	2	0.8	1	80	70
Bluefish	125	20	4	0.8	1	60	60
Catfish, Farm-Raised	130	16	7	0.1	1.5	35	35
Catfish, Wild	115	18	4	0.4	1	60	65
Cod, Atlantic	80	18	1	0.2	0	45	55
Cod, Pacific	80	18	1	0.2	0	35	70
Croaker	105	18	3	0.2	1	60	55
Flounder	90	19	1	0.2	0	50	80
Grouper	90	19	1	0.2	0	35	55
Haddock	85	19	1	0.2	0	60	70
Halibut	110	21	2	0.4	0	30	55
Herring, Atlantic	160	18	9	1.6	2	60	90
Herring, Pacific	195	16	14	1.7	3	75	75
Lingcod	85	18	1	0.2	0	50	60
Mackerel	205	19	14	2.3	3	70	90
Mahi mahi	85	18	1	0.1	0	75	85
Monkfish	75	14	2	N/A	0	25	20
Orange roughy	70	16	1	N/A	0	20	70
Perch	95	19	2	0.3	0	40	75
Pollock, Alaska	80	17	1	0.4	0	70	100
Pollock, Atlantic	90	19	1	0.4	0	70	85
Pompano	165	18	9	0.6	4	50	65
Red Snapper	100	20	1	0.3	0	35	65
Rockfish	95	19	2	0.3	0	35	60
Sablefish (black cod)	195	13	15	1.4	3	50	55
Salmon							
Wild King (Chinook)	180	20	10	1.4	3	65	45
Wild Chum	120	20	4	0.6	1	75	50
Wild Coho (Silver)	145	22	6	0.8	1	40	45
Wild Pink	115	20	3	1.0	1	50	65
Wild Sockeye (Red)	170	21	9	1.2	1	60	45
Salmon, Atlantic (Farm-Raised)	140	20	6	0.6	1	55	45
Sea Bass, Chilean	95	18	2	0.6	1	40	70
Shark	130	21	5	0.8	1	50	80
Smelt	100	18	2	0.7	0	70	60

Continued on next page

Nutritional Comparisons, continued

All values per 3 1/2 oz. (100 gm) raw edible portion	Calories	Protein (gms)	Total Fat (gms)	Omega-3 (gms)	Saturated Fat (gms)	Cholesterol (mg)	Sodium (mg)
Finfish, continued							
Sole	90	19	1	0.2	0	50	80
Sturgeon	105	16	4	0.3	1	50	80
Surimi (Imitation crab)	100	15	1	N/A	0	30	145[2]
Swordfish	120	20	4	0.6	1	40	90
Tilapia	85	18	1	N/A	0.4	50	35
Tilefish	95	18	2	0.4	0	50	55
Trout, Rainbow	120	21	3	0.6	1	55	25
Tuna, Bluefin	145	23	5	1.2	1	40	40
Tuna, Yellowfin	110	23	1	0.2	0	45	35
Turbot	95	16	3	N/A	0	45	150
Whiting	90	18	1	0.2	0	65	70
Crustaceans							
Crab, Alaska King	85	18	1	N/A	0	40	835[1]
Crab, Blue	85	18	1	0.3	0	75	295
Crab, Imitation (Surimi)	100	15	1	N/A	0	30	145[2]
Crab, Snow	90	18	1	0.4	0	55	540[1]
Crayfish	90	19	1	0.2	0	135	50
Lobster, American	90	19	1	N/A	0	95	295
Lobster, Spiny	110	21	2	0.4	0	70	175
Shrimp, All varieties	105	20	2	0.5	0	150	150
Mollusks							
Abalone	105	17	1	N/A	0	85	300
Clams	75	13	1	0.1	0	35	55
Mussels, Blue	85	12	2	0.4	0	30	285
Octopus	80	15	1	0.2	0	50	230
Oysters, Eastern	70	7	2	0.4	1	55	110
Oysters, Pacific	95	19	2	0.7	0	40	75
Scallops	90	17	1	0.2	0	35	160
Squid	90	16	1	0.5	0	235	45

[1]Varies greatly depending on brine solution
[2]Varies greatly depending on manufacturer

Safety

2

Safety

How Safe is Seafood?

More than ever, consumers are concerned about the safety of the seafood they buy at the seafood counter. They ask more questions. "Where are these oysters from?" "When did this salmon come in?" "Has this snapper been frozen?"

Americans demand—and *deserve*—safe and wholesome seafood. The government, the seafood industry, and consumers share the responsibility for ensuring the safety of the seafood that reaches the table.

A 1991 National Academy of Sciences (NAS) report on seafood safety concluded:

"Most seafoods available to the U.S. public are wholesome and unlikely to cause illness in the consumer."

Facts About Seafood Safety

The Food and Drug Administration's (FDA's) Center for Food Safety conducted a study in 1991 which showed:

- One illness per 1,000,000 servings of *cooked* seafood
- One illness per 250,000 servings of shellfish— including *raw* shellfish
- One illness for every 25,000 servings of chicken

According to the FDA, *eating cooked seafood is 40 times safer than eating chicken!*

The Center for Disease Control (CDC) in Atlanta, Georgia, monitors the incidence of food-related illness in the United States. According to CDC statistics, in the 10-year period between 1978-1987 there were fewer cases of food-borne illnesses reported from shellfish or finfish when compared to other animal proteins.

Therefore...

The vast majority of seafood in the marketplace is safe to eat. American shoppers can be confident that the fish they buy will be wholesome. However, as with any other food, seafood can cause illness.

The Majority of Seafood Illness is Associated With:

- Seafood captured illegally from contaminated waters
- Raw or undercooked seafood, especially oysters, clams, and mussels
- Seafood which is contaminated by improper handling in the home or in food service establishments.

The good news is...you can minimize the risk of developing seafood-related illness by adopting good food safety practices. The following pages provide numerous food safety tips to help you adopt safe seafood practices.

Consider Safety First...
Buy From a Reputable Source

Always buy your seafood from a reputable source. Avoid the temptation to buy seafood from a roadside stand—you might get more than you bargained for! Seafood products that move through traditional commercial channels are monitored by the government to ensure safety.

Government actions to protect the consumer:

1. The National Shellfish Sanitation Program (NSSP) continually monitors shellfish harvesting waters for the presence of pollutants and environmental contaminants. Shellfish which has received governmental approval will be labeled with a certification tag; this tag identifies the location of harvest. A reputable seafood salesperson will purchase shellfish only from approved waters and will gladly show you certification tags upon request.

2. The Food and Drug Administration (FDA) inspects seafood processors, shippers, packers, labelers, and warehouses to ensure that they maintain good manufacturing practices. FDA also monitors the quality of the products. When seafood does not meet FDA standards, it can be removed from interstate commerce.

3. The FDA also oversees the voluntary inspection program known as HACCP (Hazard Analysis and Critical Control Point). The HACCP system involves identifying and monitoring "critical points" in handling and processing seafood where the risk of contamination is the greatest. Seafood plants design their own HACCP plans and submit them to the FDA for approval. The FDA then monitors the implementation of these plans.

4. The FDA has set "action levels" for a number of chemical contaminants. State agencies are responsible for sampling suspected species. If contaminant levels exceed FDA limits, fishing of that species will be forbidden.

5. Since over 50% of US seafood is imported, the FDA monitors the quality of imported fish. Many foreign countries sign agreements to comply with US safety standards.

6. Most commercially-caught fish is captured offshore in clean, deep-sea waters. However, about 20% of all seafood eaten in the United States is derived from recreational or subsistence fishing. Very little of this fish shows up in the retail market. State and local governments regulate the status of fishing waters to ensure safety for recreational anglers.

If You Are the Source of Your Seafood . . .

Refer to Chapter 13, "Concerns for the Recreational or Subsistence Angler," page 211.

Consider Safety First...
Avoid Eating Raw Seafood

RAW SHELLFISH

One of the major causes of seafood-related illness is eating raw or undercooked molluscan shellfish—particularly oysters, clams, and mussels. According to FDA reports, 85% of all seafood-related illness is caused by eating these delicacies *raw*. One out of every 1,000-2,000 servings of raw mollusks is likely to make someone ill.

However, thorough cooking of seafood products would virtually destroy all bacteria, viruses, and parasites.

Americans have a passion for raw shellfish—especially raw oysters. Most of these mollusks are considered safe to eat raw for the majority of healthy individuals. When harvested from approved waters, the potential for illness is minimal.

On the other hand, some individuals are considered at high risk because of specific medical conditions and should never consume raw shellfish.

Are you at risk?

The *Vibrio Vulnificus* bacteria is naturally-occurring (rather than the result of pollution) and present in the bacterial flora found in warm waters along the United States coasts. Therefore, *Vibrio* may be present in approved shellfish-harvesting waters. Reports of illness are most prevalent during the warm months of the year, primarily April through October. Most healthy individuals are not troubled by *Vibrio Vulnificus* infection. However, some individuals in a medically "high risk" category can develop a severe, potentially fatal blood poisoning.

Consumers at high risk

Individuals with:

- AIDS
- Liver disease, including cirrhosis and hemo-chromatosis
- Cancer (especially during chemotherapy and radiation treatment)
- Lymphoma, leukemia, Hodgkins Disease
- Chronic alcohol use
- Diabetes Mellitus
- Chronic kidney disease
- Achlorhydria (a condition which reduces normal stomach acids)

Also at risk:

- Those taking immunosuppressive drugs
- Persons taking drugs that reduce normal stomach acid

To be safe, pregnant women, children, and the elderly should consume only fully-cooked shellfish.

RAW FINFISH
Sushi, Sashimi, Ceviche

Sushi has become a national passion with sushi bars appearing in most metropolitan areas and individual portions available in many grocery store delis. Some raw finfish may contain parasites that can cause illness. Fortunately, according to the Center for Disease Control, parasite infections from fish are rare in this country.

The roundworm *Anisakis simplex* is the only parasite of significance in U.S. seafood. Pacific rockfish and salmon are the most common carriers of the roundworm. In some cases, the worm is ingested and then passed out of the body without producing any symptoms. However, the roundworm can attach to the stomach and intestinal lining, causing intense pain, nausea, and vomiting. Severe cases may require surgical removal.

Parasites are a problem only when fish are consumed raw (as in sushi, sashimi, ceviche, and fish roe) or undercooked. Freezing at -4° F. for 72 hours will kill parasites, but many home freezers do not reach this temperature. Heating to an internal temperature of 145° F. for 10 seconds will also destroy parasites. Heat smoking eliminates all active parasites and results in a completely safe product. Cold smoking, salting, or marinating will **not** kill *Anisakis.*

At a restaurant or sushi bar . . .
- Ask questions about how they prepare their sushi or sashimi
- Has the fish been frozen? At what temperature? For how long?
- Where did it come from? When did the restaurant receive the fish?

If preparing your own sushi at home . . .
- Make sure your home freezer can reach -4° F. Check your freezer with a thermometer. Carefully freeze fish at -4° F. for three or more days.
- Consider buying candled fish. The process of candling means holding each fillet in front of a light so that any parasites can be seen and re-moved. Many processors examine fish for parasites, and consumers can ask the retailer if the fish has been candled.

Consider Safety First…
When Handling Seafood in Your Home

The 1991 National Academy of Sciences (NAS) report concluded:

"As much as 50% of reported acute fish and shellfish problems might be eliminated by more careful handling and proper preparation in the home or food service establishment."

The government and the seafood industry share the responsibility for ensuring the safety of the seafood that reaches your shopping cart. But ultimately the consumer is responsible for safety in the home. Germs can be introduced by anything that comes into contact with seafood in your home—unclean hands, sneezes, counters, cutting boards, platters, utensils, and insects.

The following tips will help you keep your seafood selection safe in your home.

Remember—Cleanliness is the key!
The most common cause of seafood-related problems in the home is due to cross-contamination.

Cross-Contamination occurs when raw seafood or <u>seafood juices</u> come into contact with cooked seafood or any other food that will not be cooked.

Cross-contamination can be easily avoided if seafood is handled carefully in the kitchen.
- Thoroughly wash knives, cutting boards, and hands when moving from raw to cooked foods.
- Thoroughly cook anything that comes into contact with seafood or seafood juices.
- Be a kitchen germ detective! Follow the germ trail in your home—from packaging to plate, brush, utensil, sink. Change sponges frequently, wipe down work surfaces with diluted bleach or other disinfectant. Don't give germs and bacteria a chance to grow!

Consider Safety...When Buying Canned Seafood

- Proper canning will destroy all harmful organisms, however, check cans and jars carefully before purchasing. Avoid any cans with dents, bulging lids, or leaking contents. Avoid jars with loosely fitting seals.

Consider Safety...In Storage

- Refrigerate fresh seafood *immediately* in the coldest section of your refrigerator. Keep your refrigerator temperature between 32° and 38° F.
- Fresh seafood should be used in 1-2 days. If you plan to consume your seafood within a week, freeze it immediately to maintain quality.
- Rotate cans and jars in your pantry so that the oldest items are used first.

Consider Safety...In Preparation

1. **Wash! Wash! Wash!** Wash hands thoroughly. Use hot, soapy water. Wash for at least 20 seconds.
Wash hands repeatedly:
   - *Before* handling seafood
   - *After* using the bathroom
   - *After* sneezing
   - *After* touching raw seafood or seafood juices.
2. Prepare raw seafood in a designated area—separate from other food preparation. Handle raw seafood away from foods that have been cooked or will be consumed without cooking. A spot near the sink works well. Keep everything used to prepare raw seafood in that area.
3. Whenever possible, handle seafood last—after fruit and salads are stored in the refrigerator and bread set aside.
4. Use a separate cutting board for raw seafood. Sprinkle with cleanser or detergent after using. Clean thoroughly.
5. Whenever preparing raw seafood, fill a sink full of hot soapy water. When you are done using an item, *immediately* place it in the soapy water. This will reduce the temptation to reuse dishes and utensils. Remember to keep your water hot.

Safety

6. Check the contents of cans and jars after opening. Look for mold. Sniff to check odor. If you notice *any* sign of spoilage, ***throw it out!*** Take any suspicious product back to the store for possible replacement or refund.

When in doubt, throw it out!
Remember the adage "Better safe than sorry."

Consider Safety...In Cooking
- Cook fish steaks and fillets at 450° F. for ten minutes per inch of thickness, measuring at the thickest point. An internal temperature held at 145° F. for at least 10 seconds will destroy any harmful organisms. Generally, this internal temperature has been reached when the fish loses its translucency and just flakes when tested with a fork.
- Oysters, clams, and mussels should be steamed 4-6 minutes after the liquid returns to a boil. Steaming mollusks and shellfish in small batches will allow heat to better penetrate the flesh.
- Hot-smoking will kill parasites if the internal temperature of the thickest portion is held at 145° F. for a minimum of 10 seconds.

Consider Safety...When Grilling
- When grilling, handle the marinade carefully. Avoid brushing marinade onto cooked fish if it has come into contact with uncooked fish. All of our grilling recipes suggest that you hold aside 2-3 tablespoons of marinade before adding seafood. This reserved marinade can be used to baste cooked seafood before serving. Remember to use a clean brush.
- Wash all utensils used to test or turn seafood early during grilling when fish is still uncooked.
- Always place grilled seafood on a clean plate.

Consider Safety...In Clean-up

- Refrigerate leftover seafood as soon as possible after eating. All cooked seafood left at room temperature for two hours or more should be discarded.
- Thoroughly wash cutting boards and utensils after preparing seafood.
- Clean counter tops.
- Sanitize sinks with cleanser.
- Wash your dishcloth or sponge after each seafood meal prepared.

If you follow these suggestions, you can help eliminate seafood-related illness in your home.

Concerns for Sulfite-Sensitive Individuals

Sulfites

Sulfiting agents are used to reduce or prevent spoilage and discoloration of food during preparation, storage, and distribution.

Source	Preservatives added to seafood. The term "sulfite" actually applies to a variety of sulfur-based compounds: sulfur dioxide, sodium sulfite, sodium and potassium bisulfite, sodium and potassium metasulfate.
Species Affected	Primarily raw shrimp. Sulfites are used to prevent the development of black spots on shrimp. Less often: raw clams, crab, lobster, scallops, and dried cod.
Potential Severity	Mild to moderate
Symptoms	• Allergic-type reactions in sulfite-sensitive individuals • More severe reactions occur in people who have asthma.
Safety Steps	• The FDA requires that the presence of sulfites must be declared on the product label. • Ask the salesperson at the seafood counter to check the label for sulfites. • Ask your waiter or waitress about the presence of sulfites in seafood served in restaurants.

Sources of Additional Safety Information

- Your state and local health departments
- The FDA Seafood Hotline: Consumers can call 1-800-FDA-4010. Questions can be answered Monday through Friday between 10:00 a.m. and 4:00 p.m. EST. Automated answers to common questions are also available 24 hours a day through the FDA Seafood Hotline.
- The FDA also provides other information and resources on seafood. Access it on the Internet at http://vm.cfsan.fda.gov/list.html

Preparation

Chapter Three

Preparation

How to Evaluate a Seafood Counter

Today you have decided to eat seafood twice a week. Hopefully, you will make it a lifelong commitment. Here are some tips your retailer wants you to know so you will be assured of an excellent seafood meal.

- Ask trusted friends and relatives for recommendations of the best seafood counters in your area.
- Your nose knows! If you smell it before you see it, walk out. Cleanliness *is* next to godliness, especially in a seafood store.

Stand back from the fresh seafood counter and look for:
- Properly cooled (iced) displays (32° F.)
- No cross-contamination (no cooked seafood touching raw)
- Properly displayed product signs, price markers, etc. (Not stuck into fish which introduces spoilage bacteria)
- Watch other shoppers. What are they buying? Ask them why!

- **Ask your retailer these questions:**
  Where did it come from?
  How was it caught?
  When was it caught?
  How do I cook it?
  Would you serve this to your family?
  Maybe they won't have all the answers, but bless the salesperson who will take your name and phone number and find out!
- Each store should offer a guarantee of safe and good-quality seafood. What is their guarantee? *Ask* them!
- Compliment them if your dinner is successful. They really want to know! After all, *you* pay their salary.

How to Pick Out the Best and Keep it That Way

Fresh whole,* dressed, or drawn† fish

Good Quality	Poor Quality
Clear, bright bulging eyes (some fish such as walleye pike have cloudy eyes)	Dull, cloudy, sunken, bloody eyes
Bright red gills	Brown or grayish gills
Flesh firm, springs back when pressed	Soft, flabby flesh separating from bone
Ocean-fresh, slight seaweed odor	Sour, ammonia-like odor
Scales tightly adhered to skin	If scales present, dull or missing areas
Belly cavity (if gutted) clean, no blood or viscera	Belly cavity (if gutted) with traces of blood or viscera

*Whole fish has head on, sometimes gutted and gills removed
†Dressed or drawn fish has head removed, guts and gills removed

Fresh Fillets, Steaks, and Loins*

Good quality	Poor quality
Bright, consistent coloring, almost translucent	Flesh bruised, brown at the edges
Ocean-fresh, slight seaweed odor	Sour, ammonia-like odor
Firm, elastic (springs back when pressed)	Soft, mushy flesh
Clean cut edges, evenly trimmed	Tears, ragged edges
Moist but not slimy	Dry or slimy

*Loin is the center cut of a large fish. Fish such as tuna, shark, and swordfish are cut into four pieces away from the center bone. Often pricy, but no waste.

Live Crabs, Lobsters, Shrimp, Other Crustaceans*

Good Quality	Poor Quality
Lively legs, move when touched	Little or no movement
Hard shell (unless soft-shelled variety)	Soft shells (harvested before molt is done)
Heavy weight (there is more meat)	Light for size
Live lobster tail curls under when lifted up	Tail hangs limp

*Crustacean is a shell-on, legged, segmented shellfish

Live Clams, Mussels, Oysters, Scallops, and Other Mollusks*

Good Quality	Poor Quality
Shells tightly closed; if open, they shut when tapped	Gaping shells; do not shut when tapped
Shells intact, moist	Cracked, chipped dry shells
Clean scent	Strong fishy odor

*Mollusks are a soft, unsegmented-body shellfish

Shucked Clams, Mussels, Oysters, Scallops, and Other Mollusks*

Good Quality	Poor Quality
Plump meat	Shriveled, dark, dry meat
Free of shell and sand particles	Shell and sand present
Clear liquid, less than 10% of volume	Cloudy, opaque juice
Clean scent	Strong fishy odor

*Mollusks are a soft, unsegmented-body shellfish

Frozen Fish and Shellfish

Good Quality	Poor Quality
Flesh is solidly frozen	Flesh is partially thawed
When thawed, pass same criteria as fresh	Signs of drying out such as papery edges
Tight, moisture-proof package	Packaging is torn, crushed on edges
Product visible, unmarred	Shows signs of ice crystals or freezer burn

Raw Shrimp*

Good Quality	Poor Quality
Translucent shells with grayish green, pinkish tan, or pink tint	Blackened edges or spots on shells (except spot prawns)
Moist	Dry
Firm flesh	Soft flesh

*Most raw shrimp sold in the U.S. has been frozen and is sold as is or thawed.

Cooked Lobsters, Crab, and Shrimp

Good Quality	Poor Quality
Hard shells (bright red for lobster)	Discolored, soft or broken shells
Picked meat:	Picked meat:
Lobster: snow-white with red tints	Off-color or dried out
Crab: white with red or brown tints	
Shrimp: pink tints	
No shell fragments or cartilage	Shell and cartilage fragments
Mild sweet scent	Strong fishy odor

Surimi (Imitation Crab)

Good Quality	Poor Quality
Clean, fresh scent	Sour odor
Pull date available	Age unknown
Firm flesh	Slimy flesh
Ingredients listed on package	Ingredients unknown

Canned Seafood

Good Quality	Poor Quality
Cans not dented	Cans leaking
Vacuum seal	No vacuum seal

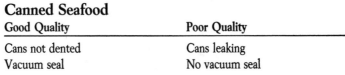

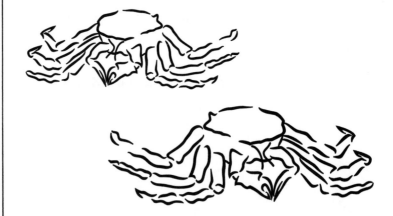

How to Substitute Seafood

Flavor and Texture of Seafood

Does your family hate soft-textured seafood? Do you love to grill fish but don't know which ones to use? The eating characteristics of seafood depend on many things: oil content, location of harvest, species, time of year, farmed or wild, and many more factors. The natural texture of seafood can range from soft and mushy to firm and meat-like. Take this chart with you to the seafood counter. It will help you substitute familiar seafood. It will also help substitute what's on sale or encourage you to use an under-utilized species.

Texture	Mild Flavor Very mild, bland	Moderate Flavor Balance of mellow and full flavor	Full Flavor Rich, bold, assertive
DELICATE TEXTURE Tender, soft, small flakes	Croaker Haddock All sole/flounder Lake perch Pollock, Alaska Pomfret Scallops Spot Sculp (porgy)	Whiting/hake Pink salmon Arctic char Crab meat Buffalo fish Rainbow trout Skate	Bluefish Oysters Mussels, blue
MEDIUM TEXTURE Versatile, medium flakes, delicate yet firm	Cod Crayfish Black sea bass Striped bass Sardines Lobster Sheepshead Sea trout Walleye pike Shrimp Black grouper	Catfish, Wild Canned tuna, albacore Canned pink salmon Mullet Shad Smelt Imitation crab Chum salmon Orange roughy Snapper Sturgeon	Canned sockeye salmon Canned sardines Mackerel Triggerfish Farmed salmon
FIRM TEXTURE Big flakes meat-like	Chilean sea bass Monkfish Tilefish Squid Tilapia Halibut Ling cod Kingklip Golden tile fish Grouper Hawaiian sea bass	Catfish, farmed Mahi mahi Perch Swordfish Tuna, albacore Drum Octopus Clams Tuna	Salmon, sockeye and king Carp Shark Marlin

Keeping Seafood Safe at Home

As you cook and enjoy eating *Seafood Twice a Week* at home, you will want to know how to keep it safe. After your seafood "catch," it will be your responsibility to keep it safe. Here's how:

Bringing Seafood Home

- Wrap seafood in plastic bag and surround in ice, or
- Carry frozen gel ice and cooler in the car. Immediately place seafood in cooler.

Storing Fresh Seafood

Refrigerator - Fish

- Remove gills and guts from fish.
- Immediately wash under cold water.
- Pat dry.
- Wrap in plastic wrap and store in airtight container.
- Ice body cavity of whole, dressed, or drawn fish.
- Store in coldest part of refrigerator at 32-40° F.
- Drain off accumulated water daily.
- Will keep 2-4 days.

Refrigerator - Live Shellfish

- Live saltwater shellfish will die if they come in contact with fresh water; they must remain alive until they are cooked.
- Immediately refrigerate in well-ventilated containers. (Live shellfish need to breathe.)
- Cover with damp cloth or paper towel.
- Store in cool part of refrigerator at 32-40° F.
- Will keep 2-3 days.
- Wash *just before* cooking.

Freezer - Fish
- Before you freeze fish, ask yourself these questions:
  What is the most convenient form of frozen seafood cooking for my family (steaks, fillets, roasts, whole)?
  What size of packages best suit serving dinner (for one, two, family-size, entertaining)?
  How will I cook it? (For instance, if you are grilling do you want to leave the skin on?)
- Freeze fish immediately when you get home from fishing or the supermarket.

Here's how:
- Wrapping fish for the freezer:
  Use wrapping materials that will keep out the oxygen and moisture, such as freezer paper, plastic wrap, or plastic bags.
- Glazing thoroughly coats the fish in water and can be done by surrounding the fish with water in a clean milk carton, plastic bag with sealed top, or individually glazing each fish or fillet.
  To glaze: dip seafood in cold water. Lay flat on cookie sheet. Place in freezer for 2 hours. Repeat process at least 4 times. A thick frozen layer of ice will protect fish for a long time.
- Label packages before you put them in the freezer. Include the following information:
  Type of fish (i.e., trout)
  Form of fish (i.e., fillets, steaks)
  Serving size (i.e., number of pounds)
  Date

Storage
- For long-term freezer storage, the temperature should be 0° F. or below. Most refrigerator freezers do not get this cold, and auto-defrost cycles produce fluctuating temperatures that destroy the quality of the seafood. For these reasons, seafood should be stored in refrigerator freezers for no longer than two weeks.

Thawing Frozen Seafood

Many frozen seafood products do not need to thaw before being cooked. Moist heat cooking techniques such as poaching, steaming, microwaving, and baking with a sauce will offer excellent results directly from the freezer.

Here are several successful ideas for thawing seafood before cooking if you prefer to do so:

- Thaw in the refrigerator (about 18 hours per pound), or
- Thaw under cold running water in a plastic bag, or
- Microwave with on-off method. Set on medium low (30% power or defrost setting). Microwave for 30 seconds, rest for 30 seconds, rotate. Repeat until nearly thawed but still very cold to the touch.

Refreezing Seafood

- If seafood thaws before it is needed, it can be refrozen. As long as you know the seafood has been held in the refrigerator for *one* day, go ahead and refreeze it. The quality of refrozen seafood will not be as good, but it is safe to eat. However, if there is any indication of spoilage, discard it.

All Shapes and Sizes

Both fresh and frozen fish are marketed in quite a few forms, and it is advantageous to know them. Pick the form suggested in your recipe or the one that seems best suited to the style of preparation.

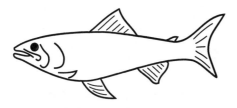

WHOLE OR IN THE ROUND

This, as the term suggests, means the fish is whole just as it comes from the water. Nothing has been removed. The edible portion amounts to a little less than half the weight. A 1½ pound whole fish will yield about 12 edible ounces, or two to three portions.

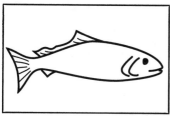

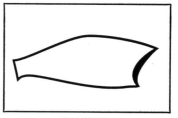

DRAWN

The fish has been gutted. The fins and scales have usually been removed. Edible portion: 50%.

DRESSED

The fish has been gutted and scaled, the fins removed and usually the head and tail cut off. Edible portion: 66%.

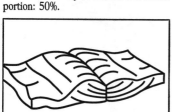

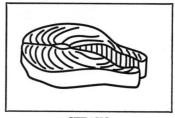

FILLETS

Fillets are the sides of the fish cut away from the backbone. They're often boneless and skinless, though the skin of fatty fish is usually left attached to the fillets. (That way it holds together better during cooking.) Sometimes small bones called pins are present. They can be easily removed. Fillets are the most popular market form in America. Edible portion: 100%.

STEAKS

These are cross-section slices, from ¾ to 1½ inches thick, of larger dressed fish. Steaks usually have a piece of the backbone in the center. Edible portion: 85%.

HOW TO FILLET A ROUND-BODIED FISH

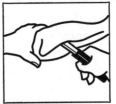
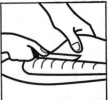

1. With fish facing away from you, use a sharp, thin-bladed knife to cut along the back of the fish, from tail to head. Make a second cut just behind the gills, down to the backbone.

2. Holding the knife at a slight angle, cut along the bone to free the back side of the fillet.

3. Peel back the free meat, then cut fillet away from rib cage. Turn fish over and repeat above steps for second fillet.

HOW TO STEAK A SALMON

1. Remove fins from cleaned, scaled fish by running knife point along each side of fin base, then pulling fins free. To remove head, make diagonal cut behind the gills and sever backbone with heavy knife or cleaver.

2. Still using a heavy knife, slice fish into steaks about 1 inch thick, starting about 4 inches from the head end. (Reserve unsteaked head-and-tail portions for another use.)

HOW TO FILLET A FLAT FISH

1. With the eyed (dark) side of the flatfish up, use a flexible boning knife to make a cut along the spine from the gills to the tail.

2. Slide the blade between backbone and flesh, lifting the fillet away from the bone. Remove the second fillet in the same manner.

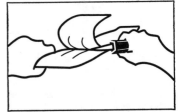

3. Turn the fish over; repeat step 2.

4. To skin, grasp fillet by the tail end, skin side down. Holding the knife at a slight angle, cut the meat free.

HOW TO OPEN A CLAM

1. Wash clams thoroughly, discarding any that have broken shells or that do not close. Wearing a heavy glove for safety, hold the clam in your palm and force the blade of a clam knife between the shells.

2. Run the knife around the edge of the shell to cut through the muscles holding it together.

3. Open clam and remove top shell. Use knife to loosen clam from bottom shell. Check for shell fragments before serving.

HOW TO SHUCK AN OYSTER

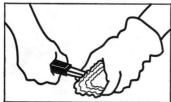

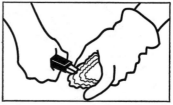

1. Hold oysters under cold running water & scrub with a stiff brush; discard those that are not tightly closed or that do not close quickly when handled. Place oyster, cupped side down, on a firm surface, holding it (with a gloved hand) near the hinge.

2. Insert an oyster knife in the side opposite the hinge, and twist knife blade to force oyster open.

3. Run the knife around the edge of the shell to cut the muscle that holds the two shells together.

4. Remove top shell, and loosen oyster from bottom shell. Check for shell fragments before serving.

HOW TO CLEAN A MUSSEL

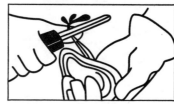

1. Prepare mussels as soon as possible after gathering. If mussels must be stored, refrigerate them at 35°F. to 40°F. To prepare, scrub shells in cold water to remove grass and mud. Discard those that have open shells or shells that do not close quickly with handling.

2. Clip or pull beard; rinse mussel before cooking.

HOW TO DRESS A SOFT-SHELL CRAB

1. Remove the apron, the segmented abdominal part beneath the carapace, or shell.

2. Lift the carapace's pointed ends, and remove spongy material.

3. Using scissors, cut about 1/2 inch behind the eyes and remove the face of the crab. What remains is the edible portion.

HOW TO CRACK A CRAB

1. To remove back, hold the crab in one hand. Pry off the shell with the other.

2. Using a small, heavy knife, cut away the gills. Wash out the intestines and spongy matter.

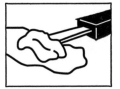

3. Break off the claws and crack them with the knife handle, a mallet, or the back of a cleaver. Use the knife to pry meat out if necessary. Twist legs loose from the body, crack them, and remove meat.

4. Cut the body down the middle, then cut halves into several parts. Use the point of the knife to remove the lump of meat from each side of the rear portion of the body.

5. Remove the remainder of the meat by prying upward with the knife.

HOW TO CLEAN A SHRIMP

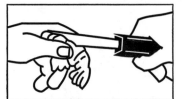

1. With a sharp knife, make a shallow cut along the back of the shrimp, from head to tail. Peel off shell and legs, leaving the shell on the tail, if desired. To devein, hold shrimp under cold running water. The water will help rinse out the vein.

2. To butterfly, cut along the back of the shrimp, but not all the way through. Spread the halves open.

HOW TO DRESS A LOBSTER

 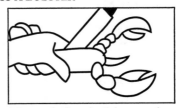

1. For lobster that is to be broiled, rather than boiled live. Cut off legs.

2. Insert a knife in the abdomen, and cut through the undershell toward the head, leaving back shell intact.

 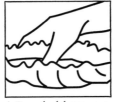 

3. Cut toward the tail.

4. Press the lobster apart.

5. Remove sand sac from head; remove intestinal tract.

HOW TO DRESS A SQUID

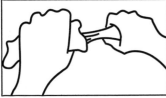 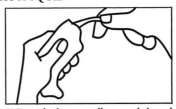

1. Pull tentacles firmly but slowly from outer body sac, leaving body intact. Intestines should come out with tentacles.

2. From body sac, pull out and discard thin, transparent quill.

3. Peel away speckled outer membrane covering sac and fins. Turn body sac inside out and rinse.

4. Cut tentacles off where they join head and discard head.

5. The tube may be stuffed or sliced, the tentacles chopped and included in stuffing or in a marinated salad.

How to Cook Heart Smart

Good news! Low-fat seafood cooking methods are often faster and easier than the way you may have cooked in the past.

Seafood will be perfectly cooked when the flesh in the center has just begun to turn from transparent to opaque (or whiter) and is firm but moist. It should flake when tested with a fork.

10-Minute-Per-Inch Rule for Fish

The 10-minute rule is one way to gauge the cooking time of fish that is baked (400-450° F.), grilled, broiled, poached, steamed, and sautéd.

- Measure fish at its thickest point. If fish is stuffed or rolled, measure after stuffing.
- Cook fish about 10 minutes per inch of thickness. For example, a 1-inch thick fish fillet should be cooked for 10 minutes.
- Your seafood does not need to be turned.
- Fish should reach an internal temperature of 140° F.
- Add 5 minutes to the total cooking time for fish wrapped in foil or covered with a sauce. Double the cooking time for frozen fish that has not been thawed.

Generally, methods for cooking seafood can be divided into two categories: moist heat or dry heat cooking.

Moist heat cooking is more forgiving. It doesn't dry the fish out as fast since it is surrounded with liquid. Cooking with moist heat is ideal for the first-time seafood cook or the cook who doesn't have a lot of time to concentrate on cooking (as when little kids are running around).

Dry heat cooking is a little more tricky and requires concentration. You will need to follow the 10-minute rule closely. Here are some suggestions for cooking heart healthy. Remember, no recipe is carved in marble, so please make these techniques yours. If your family likes a combination of flavors with chicken, they will like them with fish, too. Experiment!

Moist Heat Cooking Techniques

Technique	Seafood	Equipment	Seasonings	How To	Hint
Poaching	All fillets, steaks, whole fish, particularly low fat fish.	Deep pan, enough water to cover your seafood with liquid. Choose pan based on size and shape of seafood. Wok, baking dish, poaching pan with rack	Liquid: water, fish or chicken broth, milk, tomato juice, wine, soy sauce Flavorings: dry/fresh herbs and spices, minced garlic, ginger, as desired Vegetables: celery, onions, carrots	1. Season liquid. 2. Cover. Bring to boil. Reduce heat, simmer for about 10 minutes. 3. Add seafood. Simmer until done.	Strain and refrigerate poaching liquids when finished for a great start on a chowder.
Steaming	All fish fillets, steaks, whole fish. All shellfish, in shell or shucked.	Steaming rack with snug lid (9 x 13 inch pan with cookie rack, foil lid). Wok, lid with bamboo or vegetable steamer Frying pan, lid with heatproof plate that fits into pan. Fish poacher with rack.	Liquid: water, chicken broth, milk, tomato juice, wine, soy sauce Flavorings: dry/fresh herbs and spices, minced garlic, ginger, as desired Vegetables: celery, onions, carrots	1. Season liquid. Estimate amount of liquid so it is not touching seafood. 2. Place seafood on rack or heatproof dish. 3. Flavor liquid with herbs and spices. Layer thinly sliced vegetables on fish. 4. Heat water to boiling until steam circulates evenly. 5. Cover and steam until done.	
Sautéing	All seafood, fillets under 1½ in. thick. All shucked shellfish.	Non-stick heavy frying pan or sauté pan	Olive oil or margarine, stretched with liquid such as chicken broth or wine Flavorings such as garlic Thinly sliced vegetables, mushrooms, onions	1. Melt margarine in skillet. Add liquid and flavorings. 2. Add seafood. Turn halfway through cooking. 3. Remove seafood from skillet when done.	Make a quick sauce by adding a liquid (water or wine) to the pan after seafood has been cooked. Boil to reduce sauce to half. Pour over seafood.

Moist Heat Cooking Techniques, continued

Technique	Seafood	Equipment	Seasonings	How To	Hint
Microwave	All finfish All shellfish.	Microwave-proof containers. Microwave-proof lids to use according to desired cooking results: Plastic wrap will produce steam effect. Paper towel or wax paper will hold heat in and prevent splattering. Small amounts of foil will shield food (such as whole fish) in microwaves to prevent them from getting overdone. Wrap head and tail to prevent them from over-cooking.	Some seasonings fade in flavor when microwaved. Slightly increase the quantity of these seasonings (such as garlic, cumin, coriander, allspice). Some seasonings increase in flavor intensity. Slightly decrease the quantity of these seasonings (such as ground pepper, dried chilies, and ground mustard)	1. Arrange seafood with the thickest part toward the outer edge of the dish. Ideally, use a round container. The center cooks slower than the outside. Tuck thin tail of fillet under for even cooking. 2. Season fish if desired. 3. Cover dish as needed. 4. Choose cooking time: Allow 3-6 min. on HIGH for 1 pound of seafood. Extra liquid or sauce slows cooking time. Increase by 1 min. for each cup of liquid. Cook high-fat fish such as king salmon, trout, mackerel at MEDIUM (70%) because fat heats faster than fish. Densely tex-tured fish and shellfish such as swordfish, shark, tuna, and shrimp don't microwave as effectively as do delicate and moderately firm seafood. Microwave fish which are 1 in. or less in thickness. Double the cooking time for frozen fish and shellfish.	Use your microwave to finish your grilling. For a dinner party, start the grill early, cook the fish for about ³/₄ of the time, refrigerate it, and zap it just before serving. The microwave is perfect for single serving meals. Cook fish and vegetables on the same plate together. They are both 70% water, so the liquid content keeps them naturally moist. Always use the minimum cooking time given in a recipe. You can add more time, but you can't "uncook" your seafood.

Dry Heat Cooking Techniques

Technique	Seafood	Equipment	Seasonings	How To	Hint
Baking	All fish fillets or steaks, whole fish, shellfish.	Oven Oven-proof pan with lid	Your choice. No need to add fat. Sauces and toppings keep fish moist.	1. Preheat oven 350°-425° F. 2. Choose oven-proof pan according to size of seafood. 3. Season as desired with sauce, coating, vegetables, or seasonings. 4. Cover. 5. Bake using the 10-minute-per-inch rule.	
Broiling	Fillets or steaks to 1 inch thick. Scallops, oysters, skewered shrimp. Choose high-fat fish such as salmon, sea bass, and bluefish. Heat does not dry these types out so fast.	Broiler or baking sheet	Low-fat fish and shellfish need a marinade or basting sauce.	How To Broil 1. Set rack 3-4 inches from top heat source. 2. Preheat broiler. Line broiler pan or baking sheet with foil for easy cleaning. 3. Season fish. 4. Place on oiled rack. 5. Broil. Turn fish, basting with marinade. 6. Broil until seafood is just opaque through thickest part.	

Dry Heat Cooking Techniques, continued

Technique	Seafood	Equipment	Seasonings	How To	Hint
Grilling	Any fish fillets or steaks at least 1/4 inch thick. Whole fish. Thinner fillets need wire grilling basket. High-fat fish are more forgiving, such as king salmon, mackerel, and bluefish. All shellfish in the shell or shucked on skewers.	Grill Foil Wire grilling basket Skewers Spatula Serving platter Heavy duty hot pads	Marinades, rubs, basting sauces, any herbs and spices.	**To grill directly on barbecue rack:** 1. Medium-hot fire to grill seafood. To test heat, you should be able to hold your hand just above the rack for only 3-4 seconds. 2. Marinate or season seafood as desired. (If grilling away from home, keep seafood on ice in a cooler to prevent spoilage.) 3. Lightly spray seafood with oil. 4. If there is a flare-up or the seafood is browning too fast, move it to outer edge of grill where heat is less intense. This is important if you are using a marinade with oil. 5. Place fillets "plate side" down on rack for 1/3 of the grilling time. Turn. Baste. Finish cooking on skin side. Baste. **To grill indirectly on grill:** 1. Wrapping seafood in foil, lettuce, or grape leaves, or any other barrier between the heat and the fish will make grilling easier. However, if smoking, the flavor will not be as pronounced. 2. Indirect grilling makes clean-up a breeze. 3. Wrapped seafood in foil makes a great take-along for beach or park grilling. **To grill shellfish:** 1. Live oysters, clams, and mussels in the shell can be placed directly on the grill (oysters cup side down). Grill until shell pops open. Serve with herb basting sauce or sprinkle with lemon juice. 2. Very large shrimp and other shellfish on skewers can go directly on the grill. Baste with sauce when grilling. Cook just until they turn pink. 3. Spiny lobster and split tails will cook in 7-10 min.	Two cookie racks may be wired together as a wire grilling basket.

Ready to Eat Processed Seafood

"Quick, convenient, and tasty" describe processed seafood. They are cooked and ready to eat. Here is a glossary of some of the most common seafood terms.

Smoked Seafood

Cold-smoked

Lightly salted and smoked with an internal temperature of no more than 90° F. Traditionally, cold-smoked products have the lowest salt content of all smoked seafoods. Very moist, soft texture, mild smoky flavor.

Storage: Refrigerate (38° F.) unopened for up to 6 weeks, or for 10 days once opened. May be frozen.

Marketing terms: Nova Scotia or Nova style, Lox

Hot-smoked

Salted and smoked to an internal temperature of 145° F. or more. Hot-smoked is fully cooked. Distinct smoky flavor. May have added flavors such as garlic, black pepper, Cajun.

Storage: Refrigerate (38° F.) opened package for 10 days or freeze.

Marketing terms: Kippered, alder-, hickory-, cherry-smoked (referring to wood used for smoking)

Dried or Jerky

Seafood that is salted and smoked at a low temperature for a long time. Most of the liquid is drawn out and texture is chewy like beef jerky.

Storage: Once package is opened, eat within 3 weeks. No refrigeration needed.

Marketing terms: Northwest and Alaska natives call it "squaw candy."

Retort Pouch ("flat can") or Canned

Salted, smoked, and cooked in either a foil vacuum pouch or can.

Storage: Once opened, needs to be refrigerated immediately. Unopened, has a shelf life of many months.

Surimi (Imitation Crab)

Japanese term for minced and cooked fish. It is very bland, taking on the flavors of whatever it is served or cooked with. Ingredients such as salt, sugar, egg white, starch, vegetable oils, monosodium glutamate, polyphosphates, and seafood juices are added. This mixture is formed to resemble crab leg meat and other seafoods. Therefore, you may also find imitation lobster, scallops, or shrimp.

Crab Meat

Cooked crab meat usually from blue or Dungeness crab. The meat is shaken out of the shell by hand. This tends to make the meat a bit expensive, but easy to use.

Shrimp Meat

Cooked shrimp meat. Very sweet and pink, it is free of shells. Since there is no waste, this tends to be a good value.

Canned Fish/Shellfish

Canning seafood does not hurt its nutritional value; choose canned seafood packed in water. Many types also are reduced in sodium content; if not, rinse the contents under cold water to reduce the sodium. Also look for convenient flip-top lids and smaller sizes for a quick take-along lunch.

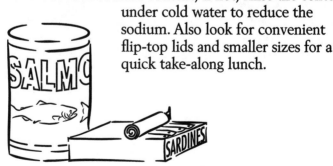

Landing a Seafood Bargain

A low-fat, low-cholesterol diet actually costs less than a typical American diet, according to Pennsylvania State University and the Mary Imogene Basset Hospital Research Institute in Cooperstown, New York. Subjects followed the basic dietary regimen of less than 30% of total calories from fat (with not more than 10% from saturated fat) and less than 300 milligrams of cholesterol per day for a three-day period. They reported savings of up to $2.24 on groceries for the three-day period. Those who made dietary changes for the worse spent $1.17 more for three days' food. It may not sound like much, but it adds up to hundreds of dollars over a year's time—not to mention all those health care savings.

Who says that "bargain" seafood can't be found? There are many ways to enjoy seafood twice a week without breaking the family budget. Here's how:

- Watch the papers for weekly specials. Usually, there is some fish or shellfish on special because it is in season and there is lots of it. So take full advantage and eat up!
- Purchase a whole fish, crab, lobster, or squid. Remember how Julia Child taught us to cut up a chicken? You can learn the same tips and save with seafood. A whole salmon can be made into steaks, fillets, and roasts for future dinners. Learning how to shake crab meat out of the shell will help you save money. The entire squid can be eaten with the exception of the beak and innards. Even the ink is highly prized. A little bit of labor will save you lots of dough!
- Stretch seafood into salads, pastas, soups, stir-fries, and casseroles. A pound of seafood can easily feed 4-6 people when it is stretched with vegetables and starches, as in a vegetable-based soup or chowder. Remember to do as the restaurants do: Serve one-half pound of the expensive seafood

such as large shrimp and use less expensive filler for the other half-pound.

"Grab and go" is the '90s lifestyle. Having convenience foods such as canned salmon, tuna, shrimp, crab, and sardines chilled and ready for a salad or sandwich will keep you from stopping at a restaurant and spending twice as much for lunch or dinner.

Appetizers

4

Appetizers

Shrimp-Stuffed Celery

¹/₂ pound cooked salad shrimp
¹/₂ cup lite cream cheese
1 tablespoon lemon juice
1 tablespoon Mrs. Dash Original Blend seasoning
¹/₃ cup crushed unsweetened pineapple
2 tablespoons walnuts, chopped
¹/₈ teaspoon salt
¹/₈ teaspoon hot pepper sauce (Tabasco)
3 celery stalks, cut into 3-inch pieces
Dash paprika

1. Combine all ingredients except celery and paprika in a bowl.
2. Fill celery stalks with mixture. Sprinkle with paprika.

Makes 8-10 servings

Substitutions: Canned salmon, crab meat, imitation crab, shrimp
Calculations per Serving: 61 calories, 2 gm total fat,
   1 gm saturated fat, 51 mg cholesterol, 179 mg sodium
Diabetic Exchanges: 2 servings are free, 3 servings equal
   ¹/₂ bread, 1 meat

Marinated Jumbo Shrimp

24 large cooked shrimp (about 1 pound)
8 ounces canned artichokes, cut in half
$^1/_2$ pound small mushrooms, cut in half

Marinade
$1^1/_2$ cups water
1 cup red wine vinegar
$^1/_2$ cup salad oil
1 tablespoon salt
1 clove garlic, chopped
$^1/_2$ teaspoon pepper
$^1/_2$ teaspoon dried thyme
$^1/_2$ teaspoon dried oregano

1. Mix marinade.
2. Add shrimp, artichokes, and mushrooms. Marinate in the refrigerator overnight.
3. Drain and serve with crackers.

Makes 24 servings

Calculations per Serving: 31 calories, 2 gm total fat,
0 gm saturated fat, 14 mg cholesterol, 112 mg sodium
Diabetic Exchanges: 2 servings are free, 3 servings equal
$^1/_2$ bread, 1 meat

Neptunes

1 7-ounce can crab meat
1/4 cup lite mayonnaise
1/8 teaspoon dry mustard
1 tablespoon parsley, chopped
1 tablespoon pimento, chopped
1 tablespoon onion, chopped
2 teaspoons capers, chopped
1/8 teaspoon salt
16 large mushrooms
1 tablespoon Parmesan cheese, shredded

1. Mix crab, mayonnaise, mustard, parsley, pimento, onion, capers and salt.
2. Scoop stems out of mushrooms. Place mushrooms *stem side down* on an oiled baking dish. Broil 3 minutes.
3. Turn over mushrooms and fill each with a teaspoon of the crab mixture. Sprinkle with Parmesan cheese. Broil stuffed mushrooms for 5 minutes. Serve hot.

Makes 16 servings

Calculations per Serving: 30 calories, 1 gm total fat,
   0 gm saturated fat, 12 mg cholesterol, 78 mg sodium
Diabetic Exchanges: 1 serving is free, 2 servings equal 1/2 bread

Skewered Scallops in Peanut Sauce

1 pound sea scallops
¹/₄ cup unsalted peanut butter
3 tablespoons lite soy sauce
3 tablespoons rice vinegar
1 teaspoon sugar
¹/₂ teaspoon cayenne pepper
2 cloves garlic, minced
2 green onions, chopped

1. Mix peanut butter, soy sauce, rice vinegar, sugar, cayenne pepper, garlic, and onions to a creamy consistency.
2. Add scallops. Marinate in the refrigerator 30 minutes.
3. Skewer scallops. Broil 4 inches from heat 3 minutes. Turn. Broil 2-3 minutes.

Makes 8 servings

Calculations per Serving: 76 calories, 2 gm total fat,
0 gm saturated fat, 31 mg cholesterol, 175 mg sodium
Diabetic Exchanges:1 meat

Smoky Salmon Pâté with Toasted Bagels

1 15¹/₂-ounce can pink salmon, drained and skinned
8 ounces lite cream cheese
2 tablespoons onion, finely chopped
2 tablespoons black olives, finely chopped
1 tablespoon parsley, minced
1 teaspoon Worcestershire sauce
¹/₄ teaspoon liquid smoke
8 large bagels, split

1. Blend all ingredients except bagels in a medium-sized bowl. Mix well using a fork or spatula.
2. Cover and chill.
3. Toast bagels and spread with pâté.
4. Pâté will keep in the refrigerator 4 days.

Makes 16 servings

Calculations per Serving: 133 calories, 5 gm total fat,
   4 gm saturated fat, 17 mg cholesterol, 398 mg sodium
Diabetic Exchanges: 1 bread, 1 meat

HINT
Wonderful for breakfast!

Clam Diggers Dip

1 6¹/₂-ounce can clams, drained and minced
8 ounces lite cream cheese
¹/₄ cup nonfat sour cream
3 tablespoons lemon juice
3 tablespoons green onion, chopped
2 teaspoons prepared horseradish
¹/₈ teaspoon hot pepper sauce (Tabasco)

1. Blend cream cheese and sour cream until smooth.
2. Add clams, lemon juice, onion, horseradish, and
   Tabasco. Mix.
3. Serve with assorted fresh vegetables and party breads.

Makes 32 servings

Substitutions: Crab meat, shrimp meat, canned salmon
Calculations per Serving: 30 calories, 1 gm total fat,
   1 gm saturated fat, 7 mg cholesterol, 92 mg sodium
Diabetic Exchanges: 2 servings are free, 3 servings equal 1 meat

Seaside Shells

1 pound cooked salad shrimp
1 8-ounce package large pasta shells
2 cups part-skim ricotta cheese
2 eggs, beaten
1/2 cup green bell pepper, finely chopped
1 small onion, finely chopped
1/4 cup parsley, finely chopped
1/4 cup skim milk
1/4 teaspoon lemon peel, finely grated
1/4 teaspoon salt
1/3 cup bread crumbs
1/3 cup Parmesan cheese, grated
2 tablespoons margarine, melted

1. Cook pasta until *al dente*. Drain and set aside.
2. Combine ricotta cheese, eggs, green pepper, onion,
   parsley, milk, lemon peel, and salt. Stir in shrimp.
3. Spoon mixture into cooked shells.
4. Place shells, filled side up, in a 9 x 13 inch baking
   dish. Add 2 tablespoons water to dish. Cover and
   bake at 350° F. 30 minutes.
5. Combine the bread crumbs, Parmesan cheese,
   and melted margarine. Sprinkle over shells. Bake,
   uncovered, 5 minutes. Serve hot.

Makes 30 servings

Substitutions: Imitation crab, canned water-packed tuna, salmon
Calculations per Serving: 89 calories, 3 gm total fat,
   1 gm saturated fat, 50 mg cholesterol, 116 mg sodium
Diabetic Exchanges: 1/2 bread, 1 meat

Herb-Stuffed Oysters

12 large oysters in shell*
1 tablespoon margarine
2 tablespoons lemon juice
2 tablespoons onion, finely minced
1 tablespoon dried tarragon
$1/4$ teaspoon lemon pepper seasoning
$1/8$ teaspoon hot pepper sauce (Tabasco)
1 10-ounce package frozen spinach, thawed
    and chopped
2 tablespoons Parmesan cheese, grated

1. Remove lid of oyster shells.
2. Place a single layer of oysters shells in a 9 x 13 inch
   baking dish. (Nestle shells in rock salt or on crumpled
   foil to secure.) Place one oyster on each shell.
3. Squeeze all of the moisture out of the spinach.
4. Melt margarine with lemon juice, onion, tarragon,
   lemon pepper, and Tabasco in a skillet over medium-
   high heat. Sauté until soft, about 5 minutes. Add
   spinach. Cook 2-3 minutes, stirring frequently.
5. Top each oyster with a generous tablespoon of spinach mixture. Sprinkle with Parmesan cheese.
6. Bake at 450° F. until cheese is golden brown, about
   10 minutes.

Makes 12 Servings

Substitutions: Mussels, clams
Calculations per Serving: 45 calories, 2 gm total fat,
   1 gm saturated fat, 15 mg cholesterol, 97 mg sodium
Diabetic Exchanges: 1 serving is free, 2 servings equal $1/2$ bread

* Bulk oyster meat or oysters in the jar can also be used.
  Place one oyster in oiled muffin tin and bake with topping.

Steamed Mussels in Beer

2 pounds live mussels in shells, cleaned
1 can beer or low-sodium chicken broth
3 cloves garlic, minced
2 tablespoons shallots, minced
2 tablespoons lemon juice
1 tablespoon margarine
¹/₂ teaspoon dried dill weed

1. Mix together all ingredients except mussels in a deep saucepan. Simmer 2 minutes to blend flavors.
2. Add mussels and cover. Steam until shells just open, about 3-6 minutes.

Makes 4 servings
• • • • • • • • • • • •

Substitutions: Clams, shrimp
Calculations per Serving: 143 calories, 4 gm total fat,
    0 gm saturated fat, 63 mg cholesterol, 345 mg sodium
Diabetic Exchanges: 2 meat

Mexican Crab Dip

1 pound imitation crab, chopped
8 ounces lite cream cheese
1 cup salsa

1. Blend cream cheese until smooth.
2. Add salsa and imitation crab.
3. Refrigerate overnight to allow flavors to blend.
   Serve with crackers.

Makes 30 servings

Substitutions: Crab meat, lobster meat, shrimp meat
Calculations per Serving: 30 calories, 2 gm total fat,
  1 gm saturated fat, 7 mg cholesterol, 116 mg sodium
Diabetic Exchanges: 1 serving is free, 4 servings equal ½ bread

HINT

*For a budget
stretcher, serve with
French bread
baguettes. Cut thin
and serve instead of
crackers. French
bread has less
calories and is
usually less expen-
sive than party
breads. Baguettes
are filling, so serve
them when you
want to fill up
a crowd!*

Hot Crab and Artichokes

Appetizers

1 7-ounce can crab
1 cup Parmesan cheese, shredded
1 cup lite mayonnaise
1 14-ounce can artichoke hearts, drained and quartered
¼ cup wheat germ

1. Rinse and drain crab.
2. Mix crab, cheese, and mayonnaise. Gently fold in artichokes. Spread in a 9 inch pie plate or 8 x 8 inch baking dish.
3. Sprinkle with wheat germ.
4. Bake at 350° F. 20 minutes. Serve hot with crackers.

Makes 20 servings
• • • • • • • • • • • •

Calculations per Serving: 59 calories, 3 gm total fat,
1 gm saturated fat, 14 mg cholesterol, 162 mg sodium
Diabetic Exchanges: 1 serving is free, 2 servings equal ½ bread,
1 meat

Salmon Pinwheels

1 15¹/₂-ounce can salmon, drained, skin removed
8 ounces lite cream cheese
2 tablespoons onion, finely chopped
1 tablespoon prepared horseradish
12 corn tortillas

Divide into 12 portions:
1 cup alfalfa sprouts
1 avocado, thinly sliced
1 cucumber, chopped

1. Mix salmon, cream cheese, onion, and horseradish.
2. Spread 2 tablespoons salmon mixture on tortilla.
3. Layer sprouts, avocado, and cucumber.
4. Roll up tightly.
5. Cut each rolled tortilla into 6 bite-sized pieces.

Makes 12 servings

Substitutions: Smoked salmon, shrimp meat
Calculations per Serving: 187 calories, 7 gm total fat,
   3 gm saturated fat, 20 mg cholesterol, 372 mg sodium
Diabetic Exchanges: 1 bread, 1 meat

Salmon Cheese Ball

1 7½-ounce can pink salmon, drained, skinned,
   and boned
8 ounces lite cream cheese, softened
1 cup fatfree cheddar cheese, shredded
1 cup fatfree mozzarella cheese, shredded
½ cup onion, chopped
1 2-ounce jar diced pimento
2 tablespoons bacon bits
1 cup parsley, finely chopped
2 tablespoons dry roasted almonds, finely chopped
1 tablespoon poppy seeds

1. Beat cream cheese in a large bowl until fluffy. Fold in
   cheeses, onion, pimento, and bacon bits. Add salmon.
   Mix by hand until well blended.
2. Combine parsley, almonds, and poppy seeds in a
   small bowl.
3. Cut two sheets of waxed paper. Divide parsley
   mixture in two. Sprinkle evenly on waxed paper.
4. Divide salmon mixture into two balls and place each
   in the middle of the waxed paper. Roll the ball
   around until coated with parsley mixture. Wrap
   ball with waxed paper and place in refrigerator. Chill
   4 hours. Serve with crackers.

Makes 40 servings

Calculations per Serving: 38 calories, 2 gm total fat,
   2 gm saturated fat, 9 mg cholesterol, 101 mg sodium
Diabetic Exchanges: 2 servings are free

Soups and Stews

5

Soups and Stews

Shrimp Corn Chowder

¹/₂ pound cooked salad shrimp
¹/₂ onion, chopped
2 tablespoons olive oil
1 cup low-sodium chicken broth
3-4 medium red-skinned potatoes, cubed
¹/₄ teaspoon white pepper
2 13-ounce cans evaporated skim milk
1 10-ounce package frozen corn kernels
1 tablespoon parsley, chopped

1. Sauté onion in oil in Dutch oven or 3-quart saucepan until tender but not brown.
2. Add chicken broth, potatoes, and pepper. Cover and simmer until potatoes are tender, about 15 minutes.
3. Add milk and corn. Heat gently (do not boil).
4. Add shrimp just before serving. Garnish with parsley.

Makes 8 servings
• • • • • • • • • • • •

Calculations per Serving: 205 calories, 5 gm total fat,
   1 gm saturated fat, 59 mg cholesterol, 216 mg sodium
Diabetic Exchanges: ¹/₂ milk, 1 bread, 2 meat

Bourbon Street Gumbo

1 pound raw shrimp, peeled and deveined
1 pound crab meat
2 tablespoons olive oil
1 white onion, chopped
2 stalks celery, chopped
$^1/_2$ green bell pepper, chopped
4 cloves garlic, minced
1 16-ounce can diced tomatoes, undrained
1 8-ounce can tomato sauce
2 tablespoons sugar
2 cups water
1 8-ounce package frozen mixed vegetables
2 bay leaves
$^1/_4$ teaspoon black pepper
1 tablespoon parsley

1. Heat oil in a large pot and sauté onion, celery, bell pepper, and garlic until tender-crisp.
2. Add tomatoes, tomato sauce, and sugar. Simmer 5 minutes.
3. Add water, vegetables, bay leaves, and pepper. Cover and cook until tender. Discard bay leaves. At this point, gumbo base can be refrigerated or frozen.
4. Add shrimp. Cook until shrimp turn opaque. Add crab. Warm through. Garnish with parsley.

Makes 8 servings
· · · · · · · · · · ·

Calculations per Serving: 190 calories, 5 gm total fat,
1 gm saturated fat, 81 mg cholesterol, 493 mg sodium
Diabetic Exchanges: 1 vegetable, 1 fruit, 2 meat

Curry Seafood Stew with Lentils

½ pound cooked salad shrimp
1 cup onion, minced
2 cloves garlic, minced
2 tablespoons olive oil
4 cups water
1 cup dried lentils, rinsed
1 teaspoon curry powder
1 teaspoon chicken bouillon granules
½ teaspoon turmeric
1 teaspoon dried thyme
2 Roma tomatoes, chopped

1. Sauté onion and garlic in oil in large saucepan.
2. Add water, lentils, curry powder, chicken bouillon, turmeric, and thyme.
3. Cook over medium heat until lentils are tender, about 1 hour. Just before serving, add shrimp and heat through. Garnish with chopped tomatoes.

Makes 8 servings
• • • • • • • • • • •

Calculations per Serving: 105 calories, 4 gm total fat,
1 gm saturated fat, 55 mg cholesterol, 103 mg sodium
Diabetic Exchanges: ½ bread, 1 meat

Captain's Night Seafood Stew

$^1/_2$ pound crab legs
$^1/_2$ pound raw shrimp in shell
$^1/_2$ pound clams in shell
$^1/_4$ pound scallops
1 green bell pepper, chopped
$^1/_2$ medium onion, chopped
2 cloves garlic, minced
1 tablespoon oil
1 28-ounce can diced tomatoes, undrained
1 8-ounce can tomato sauce
2 cups low-sodium chicken broth
1 cup dry white wine
1 teaspoon dried basil
1 teaspoon dried thyme
1 teaspoon dried marjoram
1 teaspoon dried oregano
1 teaspoon sugar
1 bay leaf

1. Wash and scrub crab legs, shrimp, and clams in shell. Rinse scallops and set aside.
2. Sauté pepper, onion, and garlic in oil until tender. Add tomatoes, tomato sauce, broth, wine, and all seasonings. Simmer 20 minutes, stirring occasionally.
3. Add seafood and cook until done, about 10 minutes. Remove bay leaf before serving.

Makes 8 servings

Optional: Garnish with olives.
Calculations per Serving: 144 calories, 3 gm total fat, 0 gm saturated fat, 49 mg cholesterol, 606 mg sodium
Diabetic Exchanges: 1 vegetable, $^1/_2$ bread, 2 meat

Manhattan Seafood Chowder

1 pound cod
1 medium onion, chopped
1 tablespoon olive oil
1 28-ounce can diced tomatoes, undrained
1 10-ounce package frozen mixed vegetables
2 medium potatoes, peeled and diced
2 cups water
1 teaspoon sugar
1/2 teaspoon dried basil
1/4 teaspoon black pepper

1. Cut fish into 1-inch boneless cubes.
2. Sauté onion in oil in a 4-quart saucepan. Stir in tomatoes, mixed vegetables, potatoes, water, sugar, basil, and pepper.
3. Simmer until potatoes are tender.
4. Add fish and simmer 5 minutes or until fish flakes when tested with a fork.

Makes 6 servings

Calculations per Serving: 217 calories, 5 gm total fat,
  1 gm saturated fat, 24 mg cholesterol, 397 mg sodium
Diabetic Exchanges: 1 vegetable, 1 1/2 bread, 3 meat

Mexican Seafood Soup

1/2 pound cooked salad shrimp or crab meat
1 medium onion, chopped
3 tablespoons jalapeño chilies, finely minced
3 cloves garlic, minced
2 teaspoons olive oil
1 28-ounce can diced tomatoes, undrained
2 cups low-sodium chicken broth
2 cups water
1 10³/₄-ounce can tomato purée
Juice from 1 lime (about 2 tablespoons)
1¹/₂ teaspoons chili powder
1¹/₂ teaspoons ground cumin
3 cups frozen corn kernels

1. Sauté onion, jalapeño chilies, and garlic in oil in a large pot until tender-crisp.
2. Add tomatoes, chicken broth, water, tomato purée, lime juice, and seasonings. Bring to a gentle boil. Reduce heat and simmer 15 minutes.
3. Add seafood and corn; simmer 10 minutes or until heated through.

Makes 6 servings

Calculations per Serving: 213 calories, 4 gm total fat,
   0 gm saturated fat, 74 mg cholesterol, 618 mg sodium
Diabetic Exchanges: 1 vegetable, 1 bread, 2 meat

New England Clam Chowder

1 pound clam meat, chopped
2 cups water
1 small onion, diced
3 medium potatoes, peeled, diced
2 celery stalks, chopped
2 carrots, sliced
1 chicken bouillon cube
6-8 whole allspice
1 teaspoon dried dill weed
$^1/_2$ teaspoon white pepper
2 13-ounce cans evaporated skim milk
2 tablespoons flour
1 tablespoon parsley, minced

1. Place clam meat, water, onion, potatoes, celery, carrots, bouillon, allspice,* dill weed, and white pepper into 4-quart saucepan. Cover. Simmer 15 minutes.
2. Add 1 can milk to vegetables. Blend flour with remaining milk until smooth. Slowly stir into chowder. Simmer and stir 10 minutes.
3. Remove allspice. Sprinkle chowder with parsley before serving.

Makes 6 servings

Substitutions: Halibut, scallops, lobster meat, salmon
Calculations per Serving: 222 calories, 31 mg cholesterol, 1 gm total fat, 394 mg sodium, 0 gm saturated fat
Diabetic Exchanges: 1 milk, 1 bread, 2 meat

* Use a tea ball to put allspice into mixture.

Seafood Taco Soup

1 pound cod
3 cups water
1 cup salsa
1 15¼-ounce can low-sodium black beans, drained
1 cup frozen corn kernels
1 teaspoon ground cumin
¼ cup cilantro, chopped

Suggested Toppings
Nonfat sour cream
Crushed tortilla chips
Shredded mozzarella cheese

1. Cut fish into 1-inch boneless cubes.
2. Mix all soup ingredients together and heat just to boiling. Simmer 5 minutes.
3. Serve with suggested toppings as desired.

Makes 6 servings

Substitutions: Crab, imitation crab, shrimp
Calculations per Serving: 175 calories, 2 gm total fat,
1 gm saturated fat, 40 mg cholesterol, 482 mg sodium
Diabetic Exchanges: 1 bread, 2 meat

San Francisco Cioppino

1¹/₂ pounds scallops or clam meat
1 cup onion, chopped
¹/₂ cup green bell pepper, chopped
2 cloves garlic, minced
1 tablespoon olive oil
1 28-ounce can crushed tomatoes, undrained
1 8-ounce can tomato sauce
1 cup dry white wine
1 cup water
1 teaspoon dried basil
1 teaspoon dried thyme
1 teaspoon dried marjoram
1 teaspoon dried oregano
1 teaspoon sugar
1 bay leaf
¹/₄ teaspoon black pepper
¹/₄ cup parsley, minced

1. Sauté onion, bell pepper, and garlic in oil until tender.
2. Add tomatoes, tomato sauce, wine, water, and all
   seasonings except parsley. Simmer 20-30 minutes,
   stirring occasionally.
3. Add seafood and cook until done. Add parsley.
   Remove bay leaf before serving.*

Makes 8 servings
. . . .

Substitutions: Crab meat, cod, pollock, halibut, flounder cut into
  1" boneless, skinless pieces
Calculations per Serving: 132 calories, 3 gm total fat,
  0 gm saturated fat, 19 mg cholesterol, 389 mg sodium
Diabetic Exchanges: 1 bread, 1 meat

*Tradition suggests that whoever gets the bay leaf in their bowl
  should kiss the person beside them or else the bay leaf holder
  does the dishes.

Halibut Vegetable Chowder

1½ pounds halibut
2 carrots, sliced
2 celery stalks, sliced
½ cup onion, chopped
2 cloves garlic, minced
2 tablespoons olive oil
1 28-ounce can diced tomatoes, undrained
3 red-skinned potatoes, diced
1 cup water
3 tablespoons parsley, minced
1 teaspoon chicken bouillon granules
½ teaspoon sugar
¼ teaspoon dried thyme
¼ teaspoon dried basil
⅛ teaspoon pepper

1. Cut fish into 1-inch boneless cubes.
2. Sauté carrots, celery, onion, and garlic in oil
   5 minutes.
3. Add tomatoes, potatoes, water, 2 tablespoons parsley,
   bouillon, and seasonings. Cover and simmer
   20 minutes.
4. Add halibut and simmer 5-10 minutes or until
   halibut flakes when tested with a fork. Sprinkle with
   remaining parsley.

Makes 8 servings
. . . .
   Options: Use white wine instead of water. Add sliced zucchini
   or use frozen vegetables.
   Substitutions: Catfish, ling cod, salmon
   Calculations per Serving: 203 calories, 6 gm total fat,
   1 gm saturated fat, 27 mg cholesterol, 375 mg sodium
   Diabetic Exchanges: 1 vegetable, 1 bread, 2 meat

Sandwiches

6

Sandwiches

Saturday Night Pizza

1/2 pound cooked shrimp meat
6 English muffins or 1 loaf French bread, sliced

<u>Pizza Sauce</u>
1 15-ounce can tomato sauce
1 tablespoon dried parsley
1 1/2 teaspoons Italian seasoning
1/2 teaspoon garlic powder
1/2 teaspoon onion powder
1/8 teaspoon black pepper

<u>Toppings</u>
2 slices onion, separated into rings
1/2 cup mushrooms, sliced
1/2 cup green pepper, chopped
1/4 cup black olives, sliced
1 cup part-skim mozzarella cheese, shredded

1. Heat broiler. Toast bread.
2. Mix ingredients for pizza sauce.
3. Spread pizza sauce on muffins or French bread.
4. Top with onion, mushrooms, green pepper, and olives. Add shrimp. Cover with shredded cheese.
5. Broil pizza about 3 minutes or until cheese melts.

Makes 12 servings
· · · · · · · · · · · ·
Substitutions: Imitation crab, canned salmon
Calculations per Serving: 132 calories, 3 gm total fat,
2 gm saturated fat, 42 mg cholesterol, 306 mg sodium
Diabetic Exchanges: 1 bread, 1 meat

Alaska Salmonburgers

1 15^1/$_2$-ounce can unsalted pink salmon, drained,
   skin removed
^{1}/$_2$ cup celery, finely chopped
^{1}/$_2$ cup dry bread crumbs
^{1}/$_4$ cup lite mayonnaise
1 egg, beaten
2 tablespoons salsa
1 tablespoon parsley, finely chopped
1 tablespoon lemon juice
^{1}/$_8$ teaspoon black pepper

1. Combine all ingredients. Mix well.
2. Form into 4 patties.
3. Spray nonstick pan with oil. Fry until golden brown
   on both sides.
4. Serve on hamburger buns with lettuce, sliced
   tomato, and pickles.

Makes 4 servings
. . . .

Substitution: Canned tuna
Calculations per Serving: 245 calories, 12 gm total fat,
   3 gm saturated fat, 81 mg cholesterol, 313 mg sodium
Diabetic Exchanges: 1 bread, 3 meat

HINT

*For barbecuing,
cook on lightly-oiled
piece of foil 6
minutes. Turn and
cook 6 minutes
longer. Salmon-
burgers are a
creative alternative
to hamburgers.
Enjoy this recipe
at a summer
barbecue!*

Maryland Crab Cakes

1 pound crab meat or imitation crab
2 egg whites, beaten
1/2 cup dry bread crumbs
1 tablespoon Worcestershire sauce
1 tablespoon parsley, chopped
1 tablespoon baking powder
1 tablespoon lite mayonnaise
1 teaspoon Old Bay seasoning
Vegetable cooking spray

1. Mix all ingredients. Shape into 4 cakes.
2. Spray nonstick pan with vegetable cooking spray.
3. Cook each side over medium heat until golden brown.

Makes 4 servings

Calculations per Serving: 177 calories, 2 gm total fat,
   0 gm saturated fat, 35 mg cholesterol, 655 mg sodium
Diabetic Exchanges: 1 bread, 1/2 fruit, 3 meat

HINT
*Kids like
miniature patties as
finger foods!*

Salmon Melt Supreme

1 15¹/₂-ounce can salmon, drained, skin removed
¹/₄ cup lite mayonnaise
1 tablespoon red onion, minced
1 teaspoon lemon juice
¹/₄ teaspoon Dijon mustard
¹/₈ teaspoon black pepper
4 English muffins, split and toasted
2 ounces part-skim mozzarella cheese, grated
¹/₄ cup carrot, grated

1. Combine first six ingredients.
2. Spread salmon mixture on toasted muffin halves.
   Top with cheese.
3. Place muffins on microwave-proof plate. Microwave
   on HIGH until cheese is melted, about 35-45
   seconds. Top with grated carrot. Serve hot.

Makes 8 servings

Substitutions: Tuna, imitation crab
Calculations per Serving: 173 calories, 7 gm total fat,
  3 gm saturated fat, 18 mg cholesterol, 500 mg sodium
Diabetic Exchanges: 1 bread, 2 meat

Open-Faced Crab Muffins

12 ounces imitation crab, shredded
³/₄ cup lite mayonnaise
¹/₃ cup green onion, finely chopped
¹/₄ cup shredded Parmesan cheese
2 teaspoons Worcestershire sauce
2 teaspoons salsa
6 English muffins, split and toasted

1. Mix mayonnaise, green onion, Parmesan cheese, Worcestershire sauce, and salsa together. Gently stir in crab.
2. Spread crab mixture on toasted muffin halves.
3. Place on cookie sheet and bake at 400° F. 10-12 minutes.

Makes 12 servings

Substitutions: Salad shrimp, canned salmon, or canned tuna
Calculations per Serving: 126 calories, 3 gm total fat,
   2 gm saturated fat, 12 mg cholesterol, 313 mg sodium
Diabetic Exchanges: 1 bread, 1 meat

Salmon and Garbanzo Pita Bread

1 7¹/₂-ounce can salmon, drained, skin removed
1 cup garbanzo beans, coarsely chopped
¹/₄ cup lite mayonnaise
¹/₄ cup celery, chopped
2 tablespoons red onion, grated
1 tablespoon parsley, chopped
¹/₄ teaspoon dried dill weed
¹/₈ teaspoon black pepper
1 cup romaine lettuce, chopped
2 pita bread, cut in half
¹/₂ tomato, cut in wedges

1. Place salmon in medium-sized bowl and flake.
2. Combine beans, mayonnaise, celery, onion, parsley, dill weed, and black pepper in a separate bowl.
3. Gently toss salmon in mayonnaise mixture.
4. Place lettuce in pita bread halves. Spoon salmon mixture over lettuce. Top with tomato wedges.

Makes 4 servings
. . . .

   Substitutions: Canned tuna, sardines, imitation crab, cooked shrimp meat
   Calculations per Serving: 248 calories, 7 gm total fat, 1 gm saturated fat, 23 mg cholesterol, 432 mg sodium
   Diabetic Exchanges: 2 bread, 3 meat

Shrimp and Tomato Tostada

Sandwiches

1 pound cooked salad shrimp
8 tortillas (flour or corn), 8-inch
2 cups shredded lettuce
$^1/_2$ cup part-skim mozzarella cheese, grated

<u>Salsa</u>
$2^1/_2$ cups tomatoes, chopped
1 8-ounce can tomato sauce
$^1/_2$ cup green bell pepper, chopped
$^1/_2$ cup green onion, minced
1 4-ounce can jalapeño chilies, diced
$2^1/_2$ tablespoons lemon juice
2 tablespoons cilantro, chopped
$^1/_2$ teaspoon oregano
$^1/_4$ teaspoon garlic salt

1. Combine salsa ingredients in a medium-sized bowl.
   Mix well. Chill 1 hour.
2. Place tortillas on serving plates. Layer with shredded
   lettuce, salsa, shrimp, and mozzarella cheese.

Makes 8 servings
• • • • • • • • • • •
   Substitutions: Crab, canned salmon, tuna
   Calculations per Serving: 137 calories, 2 gm total fat,
      1 gm saturated fat, 57 mg cholesterol, 205 mg sodium
   Diabetic Exchanges: 1 vegetable, 1 bread, 1 meat

HINT
*This also makes a
good salad.*

Shrimp Taco with Corn Salsa

1 pound cooked salad shrimp
1/4 cup lime juice
2 teaspoons olive oil
1/2 teaspoon garlic powder
6-8 corn tortillas

<u>Corn Salsa</u>
1 large red onion, chopped
1 cup frozen corn kernels, thawed
1/2 cucumber, peeled, seeded, and chopped
1/2 bunch cilantro, finely chopped
1/2 cup red bell pepper, chopped
2 jalapeño chilies, finely chopped
1/2 teaspoon black pepper
1/4 teaspoon salt

1. Marinate shrimp in lime juice, olive oil, and garlic powder 30 minutes. Drain.
2. Mix salsa.
3. Wrap 1/4 cup marinated shrimp in each tortilla. Top with salsa.

Makes 6-8 servings

Substitutions: Crab, canned salmon
Calculations per Serving: 189 calories, 3 gm total fat, 366 mg sodium, 127 mg cholesterol, 1 gm saturated fat
Diabetic Exchanges: 1 vegetable, 1 bread, 2 1/2 meat

Maui Shrimp Burrito

1/2 pound cooked salad shrimp
8 whole wheat tortillas
Vegetable cooking spray
1 cup carrots, grated
1 cup red cabbage, thinly sliced
1 15 1/2-ounce can black beans, drained
1/2 cup red onion, chopped

Maui Sauce
1 cup nonfat plain yogurt
1 teaspoon lime juice
1/4 cup cilantro, finely chopped
1/4 cup celery, finely chopped
2 tablespoons jalapeño chilies, finely chopped

1. Mix Maui sauce ingredients. Refrigerate.
2. Spray tortillas with vegetable cooking spray. Heat in 350° F. oven 8 minutes. Remove and place on individual plates.
3. Layer vegetables in tortillas.
4. Sprinkle salad shrimp over vegetables.
5. Top with Maui Sauce.

Makes 8 servings
. . . .

   Calculations per Serving: 229 calories, 3 gm total fat,
      1 gm saturated fat, 56 mg cholesterol, 214 mg sodium
   Diabetic Exchanges: 2 bread, 1 vegetable, 2 meat

Sardine Sandwich

2 3-ounce cans sardines in water, drained
8 French rolls, split
$^1/_2$ cup basil leaves, chopped
8 slices lowfat mozzarella cheese
1 small red onion, thinly sliced
2 tomatoes, thinly sliced

Sour Cream Horseradish Sauce
1 cup nonfat sour cream
2 tablespoons prepared horseradish
1 tablespoon lemon juice
$^1/_4$ teaspoon Mrs. Dash seasoning
4 drops hot pepper sauce (Tabasco)

1. Mix Sour Cream Horseradish Sauce. Chill.
2. Spread sauce on rolls.
3. Layer sardines, basil, cheese, onion, and tomatoes onto roll.

Makes 8 servings
. . . .
Calculations per Serving: 245 calories, 12 gm total fat,
   7 gm saturated fat, 49 mg cholesterol, 434 mg sodium
Diabetic Exchanges: 1 bread, 2 meat, 1 fat

Crab Quesadillas

1 pound crab meat
Vegetable cooking spray
1 cup onion, chopped
1/3 cup red bell pepper, chopped
1/3 cup green bell pepper, chopped
1/4 cup lite cream cheese
3 tablespoons jalapeño chilies, diced
2 tablespoons lite mayonnaise
2 teaspoons lemon juice
1 tablespoon parsley, minced
1/4 teaspoon black pepper
1/4 teaspoon salt
10 flour tortillas
1 cup tomatoes, diced
5 ounces lowfat Monterey Jack cheese, shredded

1. Coat a nonstick skillet with vegetable spray. Sauté onion and bell peppers 1-2 minutes. Add cream cheese and jalapeño chilies. Remove from heat and stir the cheese to soften.
2. Mix mayonnaise, lemon juice, parsley, pepper, and salt. Stir into onion mixture. Gently stir in the crab meat.
3. Spread crab mixture on half of each tortilla. Sprinkle with tomato and cheese.
4. Fold tortillas in half and press firmly. Place on oiled cookie sheet.
5. Bake at 350° F. 6-8 minutes. Cut in wedges. Serve with salsa.

Makes 10 servings

Substitution: Shrimp meat
Calculations per Serving: 204 calories, 7 gm total fat, 3 gm saturated fat, 39 mg cholesterol, 433 mg sodium
Diabetic Exchanges: 1 vegetable, 1 bread, 2 meat

Tuna Melt

1 6-ounce can tuna, drained
¹/₄ cup lite mayonnaise
¹/₄ cup celery, finely chopped
¹/₄ cup fatfree cheddar cheese, shredded
1 green onion, finely chopped
¹/₄ teaspoon garlic powder
¹/₄ teaspoon black pepper
1 8-ounce package refrigerated dinner rolls

1. Combine tuna, mayonnaise, celery, cheese, onion, garlic powder, and pepper in a small bowl.
2. Separate dough into 8 triangles. Place 1 tablespoon of tuna mixture on the shortest side of each triangle. Roll loosely from shortest side of triangle to opposite point. Place on ungreased cookie sheet.
3. Bake at 375° F. 13-16 minutes or until golden brown.

Makes 8 servings

Substitutions: Canned salmon, crab meat
Calculations per Serving: 154 calories, 9 gm total fat, 2 gm saturated fat, 8 mg cholesterol, 305 mg sodium
Diabetic Exchanges: 1 bread, 1 meat, 1 fat

Salads

7

Salads

Crab Louie

2 cups crab meat
2 cups lettuce leaves, shredded
1 celery stalk, sliced
6 radishes, sliced
$1/4$ cup green onion, sliced
2 hard-cooked egg whites, sliced
$1/4$ cup low-fat Thousand Island salad dressing
1 tomato, cut in wedges
1 lemon, cut in wedges

1. Place shredded lettuce in four small salad bowls.
2. Add celery, radishes, onions, and crab. Place egg white slices on top of salad. Drizzle with salad dressing.
3. Garnish with tomato and lemon wedges.

Makes 4 servings
. . . .

Substitutions: Cooked shrimp meat, imitation crab, canned salmon
Options: Steamed asparagus, sliced olives
Calculations per Serving: 125 calories, 3 gm total fat, 0 gm saturated fat, 62 mg cholesterol, 419 mg sodium
Diabetic Exchanges: 1 vegetable, $2^1/_2$ meat

Chinese Seafood Salad

1 15-ounce can salmon, drained, skin removed
3 cups cabbage, shredded
1/2 cup carrots, shredded
1/4 cup red cabbage, shredded
1/4 cup green onion, diagonally sliced
1 8-ounce can sliced water chestnuts, drained
1 package Ramen noodles, uncooked, crumbled
2 tablespoons sesame seeds

<u>Dressing</u>
3 tablespoons lite soy sauce
2 tablespoons rice vinegar
1 tablespoon olive oil
1/2 teaspoon sesame oil
1/2 teaspoon garlic powder
1/2 teaspoon black pepper

1. Mix all dressing ingredients in large bowl.
2. Add salmon, vegetables, and noodles. Toss gently.
3. Top with sesame seeds. Serve immediately.

Makes 6 servings

Substitutions: Canned tuna, cooked shrimp meat, imitation crab
Calculations per Serving: 225 calories, 10 gm total fat,
  2 gm saturated fat, 28 mg cholesterol, 688 mg sodium
Diabetic Exchanges: 1 bread, 2 meat

Shrimp and Broccoli Salad

³/₄ pound cooked salad shrimp
2 cups broccoli flowerets
1 cup tomato, chopped
1 cup mushrooms, sliced
1 zucchini, sliced
1 6-ounce can sliced water chestnuts, drained
¹/₂ cup celery, chopped
2 green onions, chopped

Dressing
1 cup lite mayonnaise
1 teaspoon dried dill weed
¹/₂ teaspoon salad seasoning
¹/₄ teaspoon black pepper
¹/₄ teaspoon salt

1. Mix shrimp and vegetables together in large bowl.
2. Blend dressing ingredients in a separate bowl.
3. Add dressing to salad. Mix well.
4. Chill 4 hours or overnight.

Makes 6 servings
. . . .

Substitutions: Canned salmon, canned tuna, imitation crab
Calculations per Serving: 163 calories, 6 gm total fat,
   1 gm saturated fat, 116 mg cholesterol, 362 mg sodium
Diabetic Exchanges: 1 bread, 2 meat

Salads

Mexican Fiesta Salad

¹/₂ pound cooked salad shrimp
2 cups frozen corn kernels, thawed
1 4-ounce can green chilies, drained and chopped
1 large tomato, chopped
3 green onions, chopped
1 teaspoon garlic powder
1 teaspoon ground cumin
Juice of 1 lime (or 2 tablespoons juice)

1. Combine shrimp and vegetables.
2. Mix garlic powder, ground cumin, and lime juice in a
   small bowl. Add to shrimp and vegetables.
3. Chill 4 hours to let flavors blend.

Makes 4 servings

Substitutions: Cooked crab or lobster meat, canned salmon, tuna
Calculations per Serving: 162 calories, 2 gm total fat,
   0 gm saturated fat, 111 mg cholesterol, 134 mg sodium
Diabetic Exchanges: 1 vegetable, 1 bread, 2 meat

Ginger Crab Salad

¹/₂ pound crab meat
Grated peel of ¹/₂ lemon
2 tablespoons lemon juice
1 tablespoon honey
¹/₄ teaspoon ground ginger
¹/₄ teaspoon curry powder
1 cup seedless grapes, halved
1 cup cantaloupe cubes
¹/₂ cup celery, sliced

1. Combine lemon peel, lemon juice, honey, ginger, and curry in a large bowl.
2. Stir in crab meat, grapes, cantaloupe, and celery. Toss lightly.

Makes 4 servings

Substitutions: Shrimp, canned tuna, salmon
Calculations per Serving: 108 calories, 1 gm total fat,
  0 gm saturated fat, 50 mg cholesterol, 216 mg sodium
Diabetic Exchanges: 1 fruit, 2 meat

Shrimp-Cashew Fruit Salad

1 pound cooked salad shrimp
2 apples, cut into chunks
1 cup pineapple chunks, drained
1/4 cup cashews, chopped

Dressing
1 cup lite mayonnaise
1 teaspoon lemon juice
1 teaspoon sugar
3/4 teaspoon curry powder

1. Combine shrimp and fruit.
2. Mix mayonnaise, lemon juice, sugar, and curry in a small bowl.
3. Sprinkle shrimp and fruit with cashews. Add dressing and mix well.

Makes 8 servings
. . . .
Substitutions: Crab, lobster meat, canned salmon, canned tuna
Options: Walnuts, peanuts, sunflower seeds
Calculations per Serving: 131 calories, 4 gm total fat,
    1 gm saturated fat, 112 mg cholesterol, 164 mg sodium
Diabetic Exchanges: 1 fruit, 2 meat

Garden Fresh Coleslaw with Shrimp

1 cup cooked salad shrimp
2 cups cabbage, shredded
$1/2$ cup green bell pepper, finely chopped
$1/2$ cup carrots, grated
2 teaspoons onion, finely chopped

<u>Dressing</u>
$1/4$ cup lite mayonnaise
1 tablespoon cider vinegar
1 tablespoon sugar
$1/4$ teaspoon black pepper
$1/8$ teaspoon dry mustard

1. Toss shrimp, cabbage, green pepper, carrot, and onion in a large bowl.
2. Combine dressing ingredients in a small bowl.
3. Add dressing to shrimp and vegetables. Mix well.

Makes 4 servings
. . . .

Substitution: Crab meat
Calculations per Serving: 106 calories, 57 mg cholesterol, 3 gm total fat, 136 mg sodium, 1 gm saturated fat
Diabetic Exchanges: 1 fruit, 1 meat

Shrimp-Spinach Salad with Orange Dressing

$^1/_2$ cup cooked salad shrimp
2 bunches spinach leaves, torn into bite-sized pieces
1 cup mushrooms, sliced
1 red apple, chopped
$^1/_4$ cup red onion, chopped
$^1/_4$ cup carrot, grated
$^1/_4$ cup raisins
1 4-ounce can mandarin oranges, drained

Orange Dressing
2 tablespoons frozen orange juice concentrate
1 tablespoon olive oil
1 tablespoon water
1 tablespoon white vinegar
$^1/_8$ teaspoon dried tarragon
$^1/_8$ teaspoon dried parsley
$^1/_8$ teaspoon garlic powder
$^1/_8$ teaspoon onion powder
$^1/_8$ teaspoon black pepper

1. Put spinach in large bowl.
2. Add shrimp, mushrooms, apple, onion, carrot, and raisins. Toss.
3. Combine dressing ingredients. Pour over salad. Toss well.
4. Sprinkle mandarin oranges over salad.

Makes 4 servings
• • • • • • • • • • •
Substitutions: Canned salmon, canned tuna, crab meat
Calculations per Serving: 139 calories, 4 gm total fat,
   1 gm saturated fat, 28 mg cholesterol, 114 mg sodium
Diabetic Exchanges: 1 fruit, 1 vegetable, 1 meat

Grilled Swordfish Caesar Salad

1 pound swordfish
Vegetable cooking spray
$1/4$ teaspoon garlic powder
1 large head romaine lettuce, torn into bite-sized pieces
$1/4$ red onion, sliced into rings and separated
1 cup croutons
Lemon or lime wedges

<u>Caesar Dressing</u>
Juice of 1 lemon (or 2 tablespoons juice)
2 tablespoons olive oil
$1/4$ cup Parmesan cheese, grated
4-6 cloves garlic, minced
$1/4$ teaspoon black pepper
$1/2$ teaspoon salt

1. Mix dressing and set aside.
2. Coat swordfish with vegetable cooking spray.
   Sprinkle with garlic powder.
3. Grill swordfish over hot coals 3 minutes. Turn.
   Grill 4-5 minutes.
4. Arrange lettuce, onion rings, and croutons on 6
   individual dinner plates.
5. Slice swordfish into strips and arrange over lettuce.
6. Drizzle dressing over swordfish and lettuce.
   Toss lightly.

Makes 6 servings
. . . .

Substitutions: Shark, fresh tuna, halibut, salmon, kippered
  sardines
Calculations per Serving: 232 calories, 9 gm total fat,
  2 gm saturated fat, 47 mg cholesterol, 365 mg sodium
Diabetic Exchanges: $1/2$ bread, 3 meat

HINT

*Great for leftover
barbecued seafood.*

Seviche-Style Surimi

1 pound imitation crab, chopped
2 Roma tomatoes, diced
¹/₄ cup red onion, finely chopped

<u>Dressing</u>
¹/₄ cup fresh lime juice
3 tablespoons cilantro, finely chopped
2 tablespoons olive oil
¹/₄ teaspoon garlic powder
¹/₄ teaspoon black pepper

1. Place crab, tomatoes, and red onion in a medium bowl.
2. Mix dressing. Add to crab and marinate 15 minutes..

Makes 4 servings

Substitutions: Cooked salad shrimp, cooked lobster meat, canned salmon
Calculations per Serving: 189 calories, 8 gm total fat,
1 gm saturated fat, 34 mg cholesterol, 165 mg sodium
Diabetic Exchanges: ¹/₂ fruit, 1 vegetable, 2 meat

Island Fresh
Cucumber Salad

¹/₂ pound cooked salad shrimp
1 medium cucumber, peeled, seeded, and thinly sliced
1 tomato, cut into wedges
¹/₂ white onion, thinly sliced and separated into rings

Dressing
¹/₂ cup sweetened rice vinegar
1 tablespoon soy sauce
1 teaspoon sugar
¹/₂ teaspoon sesame oil
¹/₄ teaspoon black pepper

1. Combine vegetables in a large bowl.
2. Make dressing in a small bowl. Pour over vegetables.
3. Add shrimp and toss.

Makes 4 servings
• • • • • • • • • • •
Substitutions: Lobster meat, canned tuna, poached scallops
Calculations per Serving: 93 calories, 1 gm total fat,
  0 gm saturated fat, 111 mg cholesterol, 359 mg sodium
Diabetic Exchanges: ¹/₂ fruit, 2 meat

Classic Shrimp and Pea Salad

1 cup cooked salad shrimp
1 16-ounce package frozen peas
¼ cup red onion, chopped
½ cup lite mayonnaise
¼ cup bacon-flavored bits
1 teaspoon dill weed

1. Combine shrimp, peas, and onion.
2. Mix mayonnaise, bacon-flavored bits, and dill weed in a small bowl.
3. Pour dressing over shrimp and vegetables. Mix well. Chill.

Makes 8 servings

Substitutions: Crab meat, imitation crab
Calculations per Serving: 94 calories, 3 gm total fat, 1 gm saturated fat, 30 mg cholesterol, 208 mg sodium
Diabetic Exchanges: 1 vegetable, ½ bread, ½ meat

HINT

Don't thaw peas in advance—they thaw quickly. Take this salad along as a wonderful addition to the picnic menu. Double or triple the recipe for a large group.

Finfish Entrées

Finfish Entrées

Broiled Catfish with Herb Sauce

1 pound catfish fillets

Herb Sauce
¹/₄ cup dry white wine
1 tablespoon margarine
1 tablespoon parsley, chopped
2 teaspoons lemon juice
1 clove garlic, minced
¹/₄ teaspoon fine herbs or bouquet garni
4 drops hot pepper sauce (Tabasco)

1. Preheat broiler.
2. Combine all sauce ingredients in a sauce pan; heat slowly until margarine is melted.
3. Place catfish fillets on broiler pan; brush with some sauce.
4. Broil about 4 inches from heat source for 5 minutes. Turn carefully and brush with more sauce. Broil 5 minutes longer or until fish flakes when tested with a fork.

Makes 4 servings
. . . .
Substitutions: Mahi mahi, snapper, grouper
Calculations per Serving: 170 calories, 8 gm total fat,
  2 gm saturated fat, 65 mg cholesterol, 114 mg sodium
Diabetic Exchanges: 3 meat

HINT
*Can be barbecued
instead of broiled.*

Trout with Green Chili and Orange Salsa

4 trout fillets (about 1 pound total)

<u>Salsa</u>
**1 11-ounce can mandarin oranges, drained
6 tablespoons mild jalapeño chilies, diced
¼ cup green onion, chopped
¼ cup red bell pepper, chopped
¼ cup orange juice
¼ teaspoon black pepper
¼ teaspoon salt**

1. Preheat broiler.
2. Combine all salsa ingredients in a bowl. Mix. Refrigerate.
3. Broil fillets, skin-side down, 4-6 minutes.
4. Top with salsa. Serve immediately.

Makes 4 servings
. . . .

Substitutions: Bluefish, sablefish (black cod), mackerel
Calculations per Serving: 203 calories, 4 gm total fat,
   1 gm saturated fat, 64 mg cholesterol, 179 mg sodium
Diabetic Exchanges: 1 fruit, 3 meat

Cajun Baked Flounder

1 pound flounder fillets
¹/₃ cup lite mayonnaise
¹/₂ teaspoon ground cumin
¹/₂ teaspoon onion powder
¹/₄ teaspoon cayenne pepper
¹/₄ teaspoon garlic powder
8 Ritz crackers, crushed

1. Combine mayonnaise and seasonings in bowl.
2. Spread mayonnaise mixture on flounder; sprinkle with Ritz cracker crumbs.
3. Place in baking dish. Bake at 400° F. 15-20 minutes or until fish flakes when tested with a fork.

Makes 4 servings
• • • • • • • • • • • •

Substitutions: Catfish, lingcod
Calculations per Serving: 169 calories, 6 gm total fat,
  1 gm saturated fat, 57 mg cholesterol, 15 mg sodium
Diabetic Exchanges: ¹/₂ bread, 3 meat

Spicy Pecan Crunch Haddock

1¹/₂ pounds haddock fillets
¹/₂ cup oatmeal
¹/₄ cup pecans, chopped
1 tablespoon paprika
1 teaspoon onion powder
1 teaspoon garlic powder
1 teaspoon dried thyme
¹/₂ teaspoon cayenne pepper
¹/₄ teaspoon lemon pepper seasoning
¹/₄ cup skim milk
1 egg white, beaten
Vegetable cooking spray

1. Combine oatmeal, pecans, paprika, onion powder,
   garlic powder, thyme, cayenne, and lemon pepper in a
   bag. Shake bag to blend coating.
2. Mix milk and egg white in shallow bowl. Dip haddock
   in egg mixture.
3. Put fillets in bag and shake.
4. Coat baking dish with vegetable spray. Place fillets
   in dish.
5. Coat fillets with vegetable cooking spray.
6. Bake at 400° F. 10 minutes.

Makes 6 servings
· · · · · · · · · · · ·
Substitutions: Pollock, orange roughy, salmon, trout fillets,
   ocean perch
Calculations per Serving: 180 calories, 5 gm total fat,
   1 gm saturated fat, 66 mg cholesterol, 117 mg sodium
Diabetic Exchanges: ¹/₂ bread, 3 meat

Southwest Style Catfish

2 pounds catfish fillets
¹/₂ cup Parmesan cheese, shredded
¹/₄ cup yellow cornmeal
2 tablespoons flour
1 teaspoon paprika
¹/₂ teaspoon black pepper
Vegetable cooking spray

1. Combine Parmesan cheese, cornmeal, flour, paprika, and pepper in bag. Place fish in bag and shake to coat each fillet.
2. Spray baking dish with vegetable cooking spray.
3. Place fish in baking dish. Spray with vegetable cooking spray. Sprinkle remaining cheese mixture over fish.
4. Bake at 400° F. 15-20 minutes or until fish flakes when tested with a fork.

Makes 8 servings
. . . .

Substitutions: Bluefish, ocean perch, cod
Calculations per Serving: 182 calories, 7 gm total fat, 2 gm saturated fat, 70 mg cholesterol, 190 mg sodium
Diabetic Exchanges: 3 meat

Crispy Cod

1 pound cod fillets
Vegetable cooking spray
1 tablespoon lite mayonnaise
1 tablespoon lite soy sauce
$^1/_8$ teaspoon paprika
$^1/_8$ teaspoon black pepper
$^1/_2$ cup crushed corn flakes

1. Coat cod with vegetable spray. Place fish in baking dish.
2. Mix mayonnaise, soy sauce, paprika, and pepper. Spread over fish. Sprinkle cornflakes on top.
3. Bake at 400° F. 10-15 minutes until fish flakes when tested with a fork.

Makes 4 servings

Substitutions: Flounder, rockfish, ocean perch
Calculations per Serving: 115 calories, 1 gm total fat,
    0 gm saturated fat, 42 mg cholesterol, 265 mg sodium
Diabetic Exchanges: 3 meat

Mexican Cod

1 pound cod fillets
Vegetable cooking spray
$^1/_4$ cup salsa
2 tablespoons lite mayonnaise
2 tablespoons Monterey Jack cheese, shredded
$^1/_2$ teaspoon black pepper

1. Coat cod with vegetable spray. Place fish in baking dish.
2. Mix remaining ingredients; spread over fish.
3. Bake at 400° F. 15-20 minutes or until fish flakes when tested with a fork.

Makes 4 servings

Substitutions: Halibut, swordfish
Calculations per Serving: 150 calories, 5 gm total fat, 2 gm saturated fat, 41 mg cholesterol, 214 mg sodium
Diabetic Exchanges: 3$^1/_2$ meat

I can't deny a good friend her recipe. Ruth uses this with cod, halibut, swordfish, and any white fish.

Blue Plate Special Halibut

1¹/₂ pounds halibut fillets or steaks
Vegetable cooking spray
¹/₂ cup lite mayonnaise
2 tablespoons red onion, minced
1 teaspoon dried dill weed

1. Coat halibut with vegetable spray. Place fish in baking dish.
2. Mix remaining ingredients; spread over halibut.
3. Bake at 400° F. 15-20 minutes or until halibut flakes when tested with fork.

Makes 6 servings

Substitutions: Salmon, cod, swordfish
Calculations per Serving: 153 calories, 5 gm total fat, 1 gm saturated fat, 39 mg cholesterol, 120 mg sodium
Diabetic Exchanges: 3 meat

Marinated Ginger Tuna

1½ pounds tuna steaks

<u>Marinade</u>
½ cup cilantro, chopped
Juice and rind of 2 lemons
2 tablespoons olive oil
1 tablespoon fresh ginger, grated
1 tablespoon lite soy sauce
1 clove garlic
1 teaspoon black pepper

1. Combine marinade ingredients in food processor or blender. Purée. Reserve 2-3 tablespoons marinade for basting.
2. Place fish steaks in shallow glass dish. Brush some of the marinade over steaks and cover. Marinate 15-20 minutes. Turn fish once.
3. Broil about 4 inches from heat source 5 minutes. Turn carefully and brush with more marinade. Broil 5 minutes longer. Serve immediately.

Makes 6 servings
• • • • • • • • • • •
Substitutions: Sturgeon, shark, ling cod
Calculations per Serving: 187 calories, 8 gm total fat, 2 gm saturated fat, 43 mg cholesterol, 89 mg sodium
Diabetic Exchanges: 3½ meat

HINT
Can be grilled instead of broiled.

Ocean Perch Dijon

1 pound ocean perch fillets
Vegetable cooking spray
$^{1}/_{4}$ cup dry white wine
$2^{1}/_{2}$ tablespoons Dijon mustard
1 tablespoon lemon juice
2 cloves garlic, minced
1 teaspoon dried dill weed
$^{1}/_{2}$ teaspoon grated lemon rind
$^{1}/_{4}$ teaspoon lemon pepper seasoning

1. Coat baking dish with vegetable cooking spray. Place fillets, skin-side down, in baking dish.
2. Combine remaining ingredients in bowl; stir well. Pour mixture evenly over fillets.
3. Bake at 400° F. 15-20 minutes or until fish just flakes when tested with a fork.

Makes 4 servings
. . . .

Substitutions: Shark, swordfish, marlin
Calculations per Serving: 134 Calories, 3 gm total fat,
  0 gm saturated fat, 48 mg cholesterol, 390 mg sodium
Diabetic Exchanges: 3 meat

Baked Parmesan Salmon Loaf

1 15¹/2-ounce can salmon, drained and skin removed
3 slices bread, torn into small pieces
¹/3 cup onion, finely minced
2 eggs, beaten
¹/4 cup green bell pepper, minced
¹/4 cup celery, minced
¹/4 cup Parmesan cheese, grated
2 tablespoons skim milk
2 tablespoons parsley, minced
1 tablespoon lemon juice
¹/4 teaspoon dried dill weed
¹/8 teaspoon black pepper

1. Combine all ingredients and mix well. Place in lightly-oiled loaf pan.
2. Bake at 350° F. 45 minutes.

Makes 8 servings

Substitution: Canned tuna
Calculations per Serving: 143 calories, 6 gm total fat,
   1 gm saturated fat, 73 mg cholesterol, 326 mg sodium,
Diabetic Exchanges: ¹/2 bread, 2 meat

Family Favorite Tuna Noodle Casserole

3 6-ounce cans water-packed tuna
6 ounces uncooked noodles
1 cup frozen peas, unthawed
$^1/_2$ cup celery, chopped
$^1/_2$ cup green onion, chopped
$^1/_2$ cup nonfat sour cream
$^1/_2$ cup lite mayonnaise
2 teaspoons Dijon mustard
$^1/_2$ teaspoon dried dill weed
1 cup part-skim mozzarella cheese, shredded
1 tomato, chopped

1. Drain and flake tuna.
2. Cook noodles according to package directions.
3. Combine noodles with tuna, peas, celery, green onion, sour cream, mayonnaise, mustard, and dill weed. Stir well. Place in a casserole dish.
4. Top with shredded cheese.
5. Bake at 425° F. 25 minutes.
6. Sprinkle with chopped tomato.

Makes 4-6 servings

Substitutions: Canned salmon
Calculations per Serving: 328 calories, 11 gm total fat,
  5 gm saturated fat, 27 mg cholesterol, 277 mg sodium,
Diabetic Exchanges: 2 bread, $^1/_2$ milk, 3 meat, 1 fat

HINT

Excellent in the microwave. Prepare as directed and microwave on HIGH 6-8 minutes. Let stand 3 minutes before serving.

Halibut Stirfry

2 pounds halibut
1¹/₂ tablespoons olive oil
1 16-ounce package frozen stirfry vegetables
2 Roma tomatoes, cut into wedges

<u>Sauce</u>
¹/₄ cup water
2 tablespoons lite soy sauce
1 tablespoon cornstarch
¹/₈ teaspoon black pepper

1. Cut fish into 1-inch boneless cubes.
2. Heat olive oil in large skillet. Add vegetables. Cook over medium heat 4 minutes, stirring frequently. Add halibut. Cook 2 minutes.
3. Combine water, soy sauce, cornstarch, and pepper in small bowl. Add to halibut mixture.
4. Cook until sauce is thick; add tomatoes during last minute of cooking. Serve over steamed rice, noodles, or couscous.

Makes 8 servings

Substitutions: Monkfish, salmon, shrimp
Calculations per Serving: 189 calories, 5 gm total fat,
   1 gm saturated fat, 36 mg cholesterol, 220 mg sodium
Diabetic Exchanges: 1 vegetable, 3 meat

Wine Poached Sole

1 pound sole fillets

<u>Sauce</u>
1 tablespoon olive oil
3 shallots, minced
1 clove garlic, minced
1 cup white wine
1/4 teaspoon dried dill weed
1/8 teaspoon black pepper
1/8 teaspoon salt
2 tablespoons parsley, chopped

1. Heat oil in sauté pan. Add shallots and garlic. Sauté for 1 minute. Add wine, dill, pepper, and salt. Bring to a boil. Reduce heat to simmer.
2. Add sole. Baste sole with liquid. Poach 2-3 minutes or until fish flakes when tested with a fork. It is not necessary to turn the fish.
3. Remove fish to warm serving plate. Turn heat to high. Reduce liquid by half. Spoon liquid over sole fillets. Garnish with parsley.

Makes 4 servings
. . . .
Substitutions: Pollock, orange roughy, flounder
Calculations per Serving: 121 calories, 3 gm total fat,
   1 gm saturated fat, 36 mg cholesterol, 109 mg sodium
Diabetic Exchanges: 2 meat

Quick Steamed Snapper

1 pound snapper fillets
1 tablespoon lite soy sauce
1 tablespoon sugar
1 teaspoon fresh ginger, finely grated
1 clove garlic, minced
1/8 teaspoon black pepper
1/8 teaspoon salt

1. Combine soy sauce, sugar, ginger, garlic, pepper, and salt.
2. Arrange fish on steaming rack. Brush fish with soy-ginger mixture.
3. Place rack over boiling water. Cover. Steam 10 minutes or until fish flakes when tested with a fork. Brush occasionally with soy-ginger mixture.

Makes 4 servings

Substitutions: Orange roughy, cod, pollock
Calculations per Serving: 121 calories, 1 gm total fat, 0 gm saturated fat, 55 mg cholesterol, 298 mg sodium
Diabetic Exchanges: 3 meat

HINTS
*Excellent for microwave preparation.
If you don't have a steamer, it's easy to make one. Use your vegetable steamer or cooling rack in a frypan.*

Poached Salmon

1 pound salmon, fillet or steaks
8 cups low-sodium chicken broth
2 tablespoons lite soy sauce
2 green onions, chopped
1 tablespoon fresh ginger, grated
1 clove garlic, minced

1. Mix all ingredients except salmon in an 8-quart sauce pan. Bring to a boil.
2. Add fish. Simmer 8-10 minutes or until fish flakes when tested with a fork. Serve with broth.

Makes 4 servings
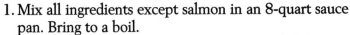

> **Substitutions:** Bluefish, cod, catfish
> **Calculations per Serving:** 177 calories, 7 gm total fat,
>   1 gm saturated fat, 44 mg cholesterol, 275 mg sodium
> **Diabetic Exchanges:** 3 meat

HINT
---
*Add broccoli and
potatoes for a
one-pot meal.*

Italian-Crumbed Orange Roughy

1 pound orange roughy fillets
1 tablespoon olive oil
¹/₄ cup Italian bread crumbs
1 tablespoon parsley, finely chopped
¹/₈ teaspoon pepper
¹/₈ teaspoon dried thyme, crushed
Lemon or lime wedges

1. Place fish in baking pan. Brush with olive oil. Combine Italian bread crumbs, parsley, pepper, and thyme in a bowl. Shake seasoned crumb mixture over the fish.
2. Bake at 450° F. about 10 minutes or until fish flakes when tested with a fork. Serve immediately with wedges of lemon or lime.

Makes 4 servings
• • • • • • • • • • •

Substitutions: Snapper, cod, haddock
Calculations per Serving: 144 calories, 6 gm total fat,
  1 gm saturated fat, 23 mg cholesterol, 123 mg sodium
Diabetic Exchanges: 3 meat

Oriental Stirfry

1 pound halibut
1 tablespoon olive oil
¼ cup water or low-fat chicken broth
2 teaspoons fresh ginger, grated
1 clove garlic, minced
1 cup broccoli flowerets
1 cup carrot, thinly sliced
½ red bell pepper, thinly sliced
3 tablespoons green onion, thinly sliced

Sauce
2 tablespoons rice vinegar
1½ tablespoons lite soy sauce
1 teaspoon sesame oil
½ teaspoon dried red pepper flakes

1. Cut fish into 1-inch boneless cubes.
2. Combine sauce ingredients in bowl. Add halibut to bowl to marinate.
3. Heat oil in wok or deep frypan over medium heat. Add water, ginger, and garlic. Sauté 30 seconds. Add broccoli, carrot, and red pepper to pan and stirfry 3 minutes.
4 Add marinated halibut, sauce, and green onion to wok and stir.
5. Sauté 3-6 minutes or until halibut flakes when tested with a fork. Serve immediately.

Makes 6 servings

Substitutions: Mahi mahi, squid rings, shrimp
Calculations per Serving: 146 calories, 5 gm total fat,
 1 gm saturated fat, 24 mg cholesterol, 191 mg sodium
Diabetic Exchanges: 1 vegetable, 2 meat

HINT

Keep frozen stirfry vegetables handy in the freezer.
You don't need a wok to stirfry. Use an electric frypan or nonstick skillet. Just keep stirring the vegetables so they don't overcook.

Bayou Barbecued Catfish

1 pound catfish fillets
Vegetable cooking spray

Sauce
$^1/_3$ cup tomato sauce
$^1/_3$ cup vinegar
1 teaspoon sugar
$^1/_2$ teaspoon Worcestershire sauce
$^1/_2$ teaspoon oil
$^1/_4$ teaspoon salt
$^1/_4$ teaspoon black pepper
$^1/_8$ teaspoon paprika

1. Combine sauce ingredients in a small bowl. Stir well.
2. Coat rack of broiler pan with vegetable cooking spray. Place fillets on rack. Brush half of sauce over one side of fish. Broil 4-5 inches from heat source 5 minutes.
3. Turn fish over. Brush with remaining sauce. Broil an additional 3 minutes or until fish flakes easily when tested with fork.

Makes 4 servings

Substitutions: Orange roughy, sea bass, flounder
Calculations per Serving: 147 calories, 5 gm total fat,
  1 gm saturated fat, 65 mg cholesterol, 334 mg sodium
Diabetic Exchanges: 3 meat

Tarragon Pollock Sauté

1 pound pollock fillet
$1/2$ cup low-sodium chicken broth
2 tablespoons green onion, chopped
2 tablespoons parsley, minced
$1/2$ teaspoon dried tarragon
$1/4$ teaspoon salt

1. Mix all ingredients except pollock in a skillet. Heat 1 minute.
2. Add fish and sauté 5 minutes.

Makes 4 servings
· · · · · · · · · · · ·

Substitutions: Flounder, salmon, cod
Calculations per Serving: 109 calories, 1 gm total fat,
   0 gm saturated fat, 81 mg cholesterol, 274 mg sodium
Diabetic Exchanges: 3 meat

Creamed Salmon over Noodles

1 15-ounce can salmon, drained, skin removed
1 cup skim milk
1 tablespoon cornstarch
$^1/_8$ teaspoon onion powder
$^1/_8$ teaspoon salt
$^1/_8$ teaspoon black pepper
1 cup part-skim mozzarella cheese, grated
5 ounces noodles, uncooked

1. Mix milk, cornstarch, and seasonings in a sauce pan. Heat mixture over medium-high heat, stirring constantly until sauce thickens.
2. Add salmon and cheese. Stir until smooth.
3. Cook noodles according to package directions. Add to sauce. Toss and serve.

Makes 6 servings

Variation: Add 1 cup frozen peas, thawed
Substitution: Canned tuna
Calculations per Serving: 247 calories, 8 gm total fat,
 3 gm saturated fat, 28 mg cholesterol, 486 mg sodium
Diabetic Exchanges: 1$^1/_2$ bread, 2 meat

Louisiana Catfish

1 pound catfish fillet
Vegetable cooking spray

<u>Rub</u>
2 teaspoons olive oil
2 teaspoons paprika
3 cloves garlic, minced
1 teaspoon dried thyme
$^1/_2$ teaspoon dried oregano
$^1/_2$ teaspoon dried rosemary
$^1/_4$ teaspoon white pepper
$^1/_4$ teaspoon black pepper
$^1/_4$ teaspoon salt
$^1/_8$ teaspoon ground red pepper

1. Spray catfish with vegetable cooking spray.
2. Combine rub ingredients in a small bowl.
3. Rub seasoning into both sides of catfish.
4. Coat broiler pan with vegetable cooking spray. Broil
   4 inches from heat 4-5 minutes per inch of thickness.

Makes 4 servings
. . . .

> **Calculations per Serving:** 167 calories, 7 gm total fat,
>   2 gm saturated fat, 65 mg cholesterol, 171 mg sodium
> **Diabetic Exchanges:** 3 meat

Salmon Nuggets

1¹/₂ pounds salmon
¹/₂ cup Panko bread crumbs
¹/₄ teaspoon lemon pepper seasoning
1 tablespoon margarine
1 tablespoon olive oil
Juice from ¹/₂ lemon (about 1 tablespoon)
1 clove garlic, minced
¹/₈ teaspoon paprika

1. Cut fish into 2-inch boneless strips.
2. Mix crumbs and lemon pepper seasoning. Roll
   salmon pieces in crumb mixture.
3. Combine margarine, olive oil, lemon juice, and garlic
   in skillet.
4. Sauté salmon nuggets about 4 minutes or until fish
   flakes when tested with a fork. Remove from heat.
5. Sprinkle with paprika.

Makes 6 servings

Substitutions: Scallops, halibut cheeks, grouper
Calculations per Serving: 207 calories, 9 gm total fat,
   2 gm saturated fat, 84 mg cholesterol, 211 mg sodium
Diabetic Exchanges: ¹/₂ bread, 3 meat

Shellfish Entrées

9

Shellfish Entrées

Shrimp and Tomato Pasta

1 pound large cooked shrimp, peeled and deveined
¹/₂ pound dried pasta
4 Roma tomatoes, chopped
¹/₂ bunch cilantro, chopped
2 tablespoons balsamic vinegar
Juice of 1 lime (about 2 tablespoons)
1 shallot, minced, or 2 tablespoons green
   onion, chopped
1 tablespoon olive oil
1 clove garlic, minced
¹/₄ teaspoon black pepper
¹/₄ teaspoon salt

1. Cook pasta according to package directions and drain.
   Set aside. Keep warm.
2. Combine remaining ingredients in saucepan. Mix.
   Heat 2-3 minutes.
3. Add shrimp to sauce and heat through. Toss quickly
   with pasta. Serve immediately.

Makes 4 servings

Calculations per Serving: 232 calories, 6 gm total fat,
   1 gm saturated fat,148 mg cholesterol, 270 mg sodium
Diabetic Exchanges: 1 vegetable, 1 bread, 3 meat

Ginger Sesame Shrimp

1 pound medium shrimp, peeled and deveined
1 tablespoon olive oil
$^1/_2$ cup green onion, sliced
2 tablespoons lite soy sauce
2 tablespoons water
1 tablespoon sesame seeds
1 teaspoon garlic, minced
$^1/_2$ teaspoon ground ginger or 1 teaspoon fresh
   ginger, grated

1. Heat olive oil in frying pan or wok.
2. Add remaining ingredients.
3. Cook over medium heat until shrimp is cooked.

Makes 4 servings

Substitution: Scallops
Calculations per Serving: 143 calories, 6 gm total fat,
   129 mg cholesterol, 1 gm saturated fat, 391 mg sodium
Diabetic Exchanges: 3 meat

Shrimp Feast in Beer

1½ pounds shrimp in shell
3 cups beer or low-sodium chicken broth
1 cup water
1 tablespoon Old Bay seasoning

1. Bring beer, water, and Old Bay seasoning to a boil.
   Add shrimp.
2. Cover and simmer 3 minutes. Drain.
3. Serve warm or chilled.

Makes 6 servings

Substitutions: Crawfish, mussels, or clams in shell
Calculations per Serving: 107 calories, 1 gm total fat, 0 gm
  saturated fat, 130 mg cholesterol, 225 mg sodium
Diabetic Exchanges: 2½ meat

HINT

*Let your guests
dig in and do
the peeling! This is
also good for a
casual family
dinner.*

"Butterfly Cut" Shrimp

1¹/₂ pounds large shrimp in the shell
1¹/₂ tablespoons olive oil
3 cloves garlic, minced
1 green onion, finely chopped
¹/₂ teaspoon lemon pepper seasoning

1. Peel shrimp, leaving shell on tail section. Devein and butterfly cut (see below).
2. Combine olive oil, garlic, green onion, and lemon pepper seasoning in a nonstick pan.
3. Add shrimp and sauté over high heat 3 minutes until shrimp is cooked. Do not overcook.

Makes 6 servings

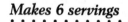

Substitutions: Small lobster tails, scallops, halibut cheeks
Calculations per Serving: 123 calories, 5 gm total fat,
   1 gm saturated fat, 130 mg cholesterol, 178 mg sodium
Diabetic Exchanges: 3 meat

HINT

*To butterfly cut:
Using a sharp knife,
cut almost through
body of shrimp
(butterfly cut).
Shrimp will lay flat
after cut.*

Crab Fettuccine

1 pound crab meat
12 ounces fresh fettuccine or 6 ounces dried fettuccine
1 tablespoon garlic, finely chopped
1 tablespoon olive oil
1 cup evaporated skim milk
¹/₂ cup parsley, finely chopped
3 tablespoons basil, chopped, or 1 teaspoon dried basil
¹/₄ teaspoon black pepper
³/₄ cup Parmesan cheese, grated

1. Cook fettuccine according to package directions.
2. While fettuccine cooks, sauté garlic in oil in a large skillet. Add skim milk and heat through.
3. Stir in crab, parsley, basil, and pepper. Continue heating.
4. Add drained fettuccine and Parmesan cheese. Toss lightly and serve immediately.

Makes 8 servings

Substitutions: Clams, scallops, shrimp
Calculations per Serving: 219 calories, 6 gm total fat,
  2 gm saturated fat, 42 mg cholesterol, 383 mg sodium
Diabetic Exchanges: 1 vegetable, 1 bread, 3 meat

Stuffed Italian Squid Manicotti

12 large whole squid

Sauce
$^1/_2$ cup onion, chopped
1 clove garlic, minced
2 tablespoons olive oil
1 15$^1/_2$-ounce can Italian stewed tomatoes
$^1/_8$ teaspoon lemon pepper seasoning

Stuffing
16 ounces part-skim ricotta cheese
$^1/_4$ cup parsley, chopped
$^1/_4$ cup black olives, chopped
$^1/_2$ cup bread crumbs

1. Clean squid, leaving mantles (bodies) whole for stuffing. Remove tentacles from squid. Chop and reserve for stuffing.
2. Sauté onion and garlic in oil until lightly browned. Add stewed tomatoes and lemon pepper seasoning. Cover and simmer 10 minutes or until sauce is thick. Set aside.
3. Combine chopped tentacles, ricotta cheese, parsley, olives, and bread crumbs in a separate bowl. Fill the squid with stuffing. Close ends and secure with toothpicks.
4. Place filled squid in large, 2-inch deep baking dish and pour sauce on top. Bake at 425° F. 20-25 minutes.

Makes 6 servings

Calculations per Serving: 298 calories, 13 gm total fat, 5 gm saturated fat, 288 mg cholesterol, 450 mg sodium
Diabetic Exchanges: 1 bread, 3$^1/_2$ meat

Lobster Beach Bake

2 live lobsters, 1¹/₄ pounds each
2 quarts water, or enough to cover all ingredients
¹/₂ teaspoon salt
2 ears sweet corn, shucked
2 small boiling onions, skins removed
6 small red potatoes, scrubbed

1. In a 6-quart pan, bring water and salt to a boil. Place vegetables into boiling water. Cover and simmer 8 minutes.
2. Plunge lobster into water with vegetables (add more hot water if necessary). Return water to boiling. Cover. Reduce heat and simmer lobster (18 minutes for the first pound, 3 minutes for each additional pound). Start timing when you first see steam from pot.
3. Pull lobster from pot, drain, and cool 5-10 minutes.
4. Remove vegetables just before serving.

Makes 2 servings

Calculations per Serving: 324 calories, 2 gm total fat, 0 gm saturated fat, 81 mg cholesterol, 397 mg sodium
Diabetic Exchanges: 4 bread, 3 meat

Whole Live Lobster

The two most common ways to cook live lobsters are steaming and boiling.

To steam lobsters: Put about 2 inches of salted water in the bottom of a large kettle. Bring the water to a rolling boil and put in the live lobsters, one at a time. Cover kettle, return water to boiling and begin timing. Reduce heat and simmer. Allow 18 minutes for 1 to 1¼ pound hard-shell lobsters.

To boil lobsters: Fill a large kettle ¾ full with salted water. If sea water is not available, add 2 tablespoons salt for each quart of water. A good rule of thumb is to allow 2½ quarts of water for each lobster. Bring the water to a boil. Put in the live lobsters one at a time and let the water boil again. Cover kettle and simmer about 15 minutes for 1 to 1¼ pound hard-shell lobsters.

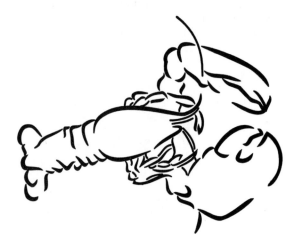

If the lobster is a new shell lobster with a soft shell, reduce boiling or steaming time by 3 minutes.

Crack and Enjoy!
When the antennae pull out easily, the lobsters are done.

1. Twist off the large claws and crack open.
2. Separate the tail from the body and break off the tail flippers.
3. Insert a fork and push the tail meat out in one piece. Remove and discard the black vein which runs the entire length of the tail meat.
4. Open the body by cracking it apart sideways. Lobster meat lies in the four pockets where the small walking legs are attached. The small walking legs also contain excellent meat which can be removed by sucking on the ends of the legs.

Makes 1 serving

Calculations per Serving: 102 calories, 1 gm total fat, 0 gm saturated fat, 107 mg cholesterol, 335 mg sodium
Diabetic Exchanges: 3 meat

Shellfish Entrées

HINT
Make a complete meal by adding vegetables to the kettle. Red potatoes, carrots, sweet corn, and boiling onions are tasty.

Squid Sauté

1 pound squid strips or rings
¹/₄ cup low-sodium chicken broth
¹/₄ cup water
1 tablespoon olive oil
1 teaspoon fresh ginger, grated, or ¹/₄ teaspoon
    ground ginger
1 teaspoon lemon peel, grated
¹/₄ teaspoon lemon pepper seasoning
1 cup carrots, sliced
1 cup celery, sliced
1 cup green onion, diagonally sliced
1 cup broccoli flowerets
1 cup mushrooms, sliced

1. Combine chicken broth, water, oil, ginger, lemon
   peel, and lemon pepper seasoning in large frying pan.
   Heat. Add vegetables. Sauté until tender-crisp.
2. Add squid to pan.
3. Sauté 2 minutes. Serve immediately.

Makes 4 servings
. . . .
Substitutions: Scallops, monkfish medallions, halibut cheeks
Calculations per Serving: 184 calories, 5 gm total fat, 1 gm
    saturated fat, 264 mg cholesterol, 182 mg sodium,
Diabetic Exchanges: 1 bread, 3 meat

Summertime Crab Enchiladas

1 pound imitation crab, diced
1 cup small red onion, chopped
1 cup Roma tomatoes, diced
1/2 cup cucumber, diced
1/4 cup cilantro, chopped
1 cup nonfat sour cream
1 small avocado, sliced
12 corn tortillas
Salsa

1. In medium bowl, mix crab, onion, tomato, cucumber, cilantro, and sour cream.
2. Toss gently to combine without breaking up the crab.
3. Spread each tortilla with about 2-3 tablespoons crab filling. Roll. Garnish with a sliced avocado. Serve with salsa.

Makes 12 servings
• • • • • • • • • • •
Substitution: Shrimp, crab meat
Calculations per Serving: 242 calories, 8 gm total fat, 3 gm saturated fat, 22 mg cholesterol, 202 mg sodium
Diabetic Exchanges: 1/2 bread, 1 vegetable, 2 meat

HINT
A family favorite on a hot day!

Broiled Sesame Scallops

1 pound sea scallops
2 tablespoons sesame seeds, toasted
2 tablespoons lite soy sauce
2 tablespoons dry sherry
2 green onions, chopped
1 teaspoon brown sugar
1 clove garlic, minced
$^1/_2$ teaspoon ground ginger
$^1/_8$ teaspoon black pepper

1. Combine all ingredients except the scallops in a large bowl.
2. Stir in scallops.
3. Place scallops on foil-lined broiler pan. Broil 3-4 minutes.

Makes 4 servings

Substitutions: Large shrimp, halibut cheeks
Calculations per Serving: 161 calories, 4 gm total fat,
  0 gm saturated fat, 60 mg cholesterol, 433 mg sodium
Diabetic Exchanges: $3^1/_2$ meat

Elegant Scallops

1 pound sea scallops
$^1/_2$ tablespoon olive oil
$^1/_2$ tablespoon margarine
$^1/_2$ cup mushrooms, thinly sliced
$^1/_4$ cup green onion, minced
1 clove garlic, minced
$^1/_4$ teaspoon pepper
$^1/_4$ teaspoon salt
$^1/_4$ cup dry sherry
$^1/_4$ cup parsley, chopped

1. Heat oil and margarine in a large frying pan. Add mushrooms, onion, garlic, pepper, and salt. Sauté until mushrooms are tender.
2. Add scallops and sherry. Cook over very high heat until sherry is reduced by half. When finished, there should be only a very light brown sauce glazing the scallops.
3. Sprinkle with parsley.

Makes 4 servings

Substitutions: Monkfish medallions, halibut cubes, peeled and deveined shrimp
Calculations per Serving: 167 calories, 4 gm total fat, 1 gm saturated fat, 39 mg cholesterol, 241 mg sodium
Diabetic Exchanges: $^1/_2$ bread, 3 meat

Scallops Almandine

1 pound sea scallops
1/4 teaspoon salt
1/4 teaspoon pepper
1/2 cup bread crumbs
1 tablespoon butter
1/2 cup slivered almonds
2 tablespoons parsley, chopped

1. Rinse scallops in cold water. Pat dry with paper towels.
   Sprinkle with salt and pepper. Roll in bread crumbs.
2. Melt butter in skillet. Add scallops and sauté over
   high heat, browning them well on both sides. Total
   cooking time is approximately 4 minutes.
3. Garnish with almonds and parsley. Serve immediately.

Makes 4 servings
. . . .
Substitutions: Oysters, shrimp
Calculations per Serving: 260 calories, 12 gm total fat,
    3 gm saturated fat, 45 mg cholesterol, 439 mg sodium
Diabetic Exchanges: 1 bread, 3 meat

Steamed Clams

2 pounds in-shell clams
1 cup low-sodium chicken broth
1 cup white wine
1 cup water
1/4 cup celery, chopped
1/4 cup green onion, chopped
1/4 cup carrot, chopped
2 cloves garlic, minced
1 teaspoon dried thyme
4 drops hot pepper sauce (Tabasco)

1. Scrub clams in cold water just before cooking.
2. Combine remaining ingredients in a deep pan.
3. Bring to a boil. Add clams. Cover and simmer until shells open. Steam 4-6 minutes longer.

Makes 4 servings

Substitutions: Cockles, mussels, scallops
Calculations per Serving: 111 calories, 1 gm total fat,
  0 gm saturated fat, 24 mg cholesterol, 143 mg sodium,
Diabetic Exchanges: 2 meat

HINT
Don't throw out the broth. It's delicious! Serve bread along-side so you can soak up the juice. Or refrigerate the broth for 2 days or freeze and use as a clam chowder base. It also makes a wonderful poaching base for salmon.

Spicy Steamed Mussels

2 pounds mussels, debearded
1 cup white wine
2 Roma tomatoes, diced
¹/₄ cup parsley, chopped
2 tablespoons shallots, chopped
1 tablespoon olive oil
3 cloves garlic, minced
¹/₄ teaspoon dried red pepper flakes
¹/₄ teaspoon dried oregano

1. Mix all ingredients except mussels in a deep saucepan. Simmer 2 minutes to blend flavors.
2. Add mussels to saucepan and cover.
3. Steam until shells just open. Continue steaming 4-6 minutes.

Serves 4
. . . .
Substitution: Clams, cockles
Calculations per Serving: 132 calories, 3 gm total fat,
    0 gm saturated fat, 40 mg cholesterol, 208 mg sodium
Diabetic Exchanges: 2 meat

Oyster Sauté

1¹/₂ pounds small oysters, shucked (2 8-ounce
  jars small oysters)
1 tablespoon olive oil
¹/₂ cup green onion, chopped
¹/₂ cup red or green bell pepper, finely chopped
¹/₃ cup celery, chopped
¹/₂ cup low-sodium chicken broth
1 teaspoon dried dill weed
1 tablespoon parsley, chopped
Squeeze of lemon

1. Heat olive oil in skillet, then add vegetables and
   chicken broth. Sauté until tender-crisp.
2. Add oysters and dill weed. Sauté 4-6 minutes.
3. Sprinkle with parsley and squeeze of lemon.

Makes 4 servings

Substitutions: Shrimp, scallops
Calculations per Serving: 85 calories, 4 gm total fat,
  1 gm saturated fat, 33 mg cholesterol, 110 mg sodium
Diabetic Exchanges: 1 vegetable, 1 meat

Breaded Oysters Parmesan

1 10-ounce jar small oysters
$^{1}/_{4}$ cup green onion, chopped
$^{1}/_{4}$ cup fresh parsley, chopped
3 cloves garlic, minced
1 tablespoon olive oil
1 tablespoon lime juice
4 drops hot pepper sauce (Tabasco)
$^{1}/_{4}$ cup Parmesan cheese, grated
$^{1}/_{4}$ cup bread crumbs
$^{1}/_{4}$ teaspoon black pepper

1. Rinse oysters and pat dry.
2. Place green onion, parsley, garlic, oil, lime juice, and Tabasco in nonstick frying pan. Sauté for 3 minutes.
3. Mix cheese, bread crumbs, and pepper in a small bowl. Roll oysters in cheese mixture.
4. Sauté for 4-6 minutes in vegetables.

Makes 2-4 servings

Substitution: Scallops
Calculations per Serving: 148 calories, 7 gm total fat, 2 gm saturated fat, 40 mg cholesterol, 245 mg sodium
Diabetic Exchanges: $^{1}/_{2}$ bread, 2 meat

Salsa Baked Oysters in the Shell

30 oysters in the shell
4 cups rock salt*
$^1/_3$ cup bread crumbs
$^1/_2$ cup salsa
$^1/_2$ cup mozzarella cheese, grated

1. Sprinkle rock salt in two 9 x 13 inch baking pans.
2. Shuck oysters, leaving meat in cup side of shell. Nestle oyster shells in rock salt.
3. Mix bread crumbs with salsa and cheese. Spread on top of oysters in shell.
4. Bake at 400° F. 8-10 minutes or until hot and bubbly. Serve immediately.

Makes 6 servings

Calculations per Serving: 110 calories, 4 gm total fat, 2 gm saturated fat, 43 mg cholesterol, 313 mg sodium
Diabetic Exchanges: $^1/_2$ bread, 1 meat

HINT

To shuck oysters, use an oyster knife.
*Rock salt helps keep oysters upright while baking.
A large sheet of crinkled foil set in the bottom of each baking pan can be used in place of the salt.

Baked Seafood Linguine

2 cups crab meat (or 2 6½-ounce cans)
8 ounces linguine, uncooked
½ pound mushrooms, sliced
¼ cup onion, chopped
1 tablespoon margarine
1 cup white wine
½ cup low-sodium chicken broth
¼ cup water
3 tablespoons flour
⅛ teaspoon black pepper
½ cup nonfat sour cream
½ cup low-fat Monterey Jack cheese, shredded
Vegetable cooking spray

<u>Topping</u>
¼ cup bread crumbs
2 tablespoons Parmesan cheese, grated

1. Cook linguine according to package directions. Drain. Set aside
2. Sauté mushrooms and onions in margarine.
3. Combine wine, chicken broth, water, flour, and pepper in a bowl and stir to mix. Add to vegetables. Cook over medium heat until thickened. Remove from heat. Gently stir in crab, sour cream, and cheese.
4. Mix noodles with sauce.
5. Coat 9 x 13 inch casserole dish with vegetable cooking spray. Pour mixture into dish.
6. Combine bread crumbs and Parmesan cheese. Sprinkle over casserole. Bake, uncovered, at 350° F. 30 minutes.

Serves 6

Calculations per Serving: 357 calories, 12 gm total fat,
   5 gm saturated fat, 46 mg cholesterol, 310 mg sodium
Diabetic Exchanges: 2 bread, 2 meat, 1 fat

Microwave

10

Microwave

Salmon Florentine

1 pound salmon fillets or steaks
4 cups packed spinach leaves (about 8 ounces), or
    8 ounces frozen spinach, thawed and drained
1 medium onion, chopped
1 tablespoon olive oil
1 teaspoon lemon juice
$^{1}/_{2}$ teaspoon soy sauce
$^{1}/_{4}$ teaspoon sugar
$^{1}/_{4}$ teaspoon black pepper

1. Place spinach and onion on large microwave-proof
   serving platter. Cover with plastic wrap and microwave on HIGH 3 minutes. Place salmon over spinach
   mixture.
2. Combine remaining ingredients in a small bowl.
   Drizzle over spinach and salmon.
3. Cover with plastic wrap; turn back one corner. Microwave on MEDIUM 4-6 minutes or until fish flakes
   when tested with a fork. Let stand 1-2 minutes to
   complete cooking.

Makes 4 servings

Substitutions: Ocean perch, orange roughy, bluefish, trout
Calculations per Serving: 188 calories, 8 gm total fat,
    1 gm saturated fat, 84 mg cholesterol, 147 mg sodium
Diabetic Exchanges: $3^{1}/_{2}$ meat

Cod Veracruz

1 pound cod fillets
1/4 cup mushrooms, sliced
1/4 cup onion, chopped
1/4 cup celery, diced
1 tablespoon lemon juice
1 tablespoon vegetable oil
1/4 teaspoon dried thyme
1/4 teaspoon black pepper
1 medium tomato, diced
Parsley sprigs

1. Combine mushrooms, onion, celery, lemon juice, oil, thyme, and pepper in microwave-proof bowl. Microwave on HIGH 2-3 minutes or until tender-crisp.
2. Lay cod fillets in microwave-proof dish. Spoon vegetable mixture over fish. Add tomatoes. Cover dish with plastic wrap; turn back one corner.
3. Microwave on HIGH 3-5 minutes or until fish just flakes when tested with fork. Let stand 1-2 minutes to complete cooking. Garnish with parsley.

Makes 4 servings
· · · · · · · · · · · ·

Substitution: Orange roughy
Calculations per Serving: 141 calories, 4 gm total fat,
   0 gm saturated fat, 49 mg cholesterol, 76 mg sodium
Diabetic Exchanges: 3 meat

One-Dish Halibut

1 pound halibut fillets or steaks
1 pound mixed frozen vegetables
$1/4$ cup lemon juice
1 tablespoon olive oil
$1/4$ teaspoon lemon pepper seasoning
1 Roma tomato, diced
$1/4$ cup parsley, chopped

1. Place vegetables in a microwave-proof baking dish. Cover dish with plastic wrap; turn back one corner. Microwave on HIGH 2 $1/2$ minutes. Stir. Lay halibut over vegetables.
2. Mix lemon juice, olive oil, and lemon pepper seasoning in a small bowl. Pour over fish.
3. Cover dish with microwave wrap. Turn back one corner and microwave on HIGH 4-5 minutes or until fish just flakes when tested with a fork. Let stand 1-2 minutes to complete cooking.
4. Garnish with tomato and parsley.

Makes 4 servings

Substitutions: Orange roughy, flounder, salmon
Calculations per Serving: 231 calories, 6 gm total fat,
  1 gm saturated fat, 36 mg cholesterol, 142 mg sodium
Diabetic Exchanges: 1 bread, 3 meat

Caribbean Haddock

$^1/_2$ pound haddock fillets
1 teaspoon margarine
1 small orange, peeled, seeded, and diced
$^1/_2$ medium onion, diced
1 tablespoon lemon juice
2 teaspoons parsley, minced
$^1/_4$ teaspoon salt
$^1/_4$ teaspoon black pepper
$^1/_8$ teaspoon nutmeg
$^1/_8$ teaspoon cinnamon

1. Melt margarine in microwave-proof dish. Combine remaining ingredients except haddock in a separate bowl and mix. Add fish to bowl and turn to coat on all sides. Carefully place fillets in margerine and cover dish with plastic wrap; turn back one corner.
2. Microwave on HIGH 4-6 minutes until fish just flakes when tested with a fork.
3. Let stand 1-2 minutes to complete cooking.

Makes 2 servings

Substitutions: Cod, orange roughy, halibut
Calculations per Serving: 171 calories, 3 gm total fat,
   1 gm saturated fat, 65 mg cholesterol, 346 mg sodium
Diabetic Exchanges: 1 fruit, 3 meat

Trout with Cucumber Sauce

1¹/₂ pounds trout fillets
1 medium onion, thinly sliced
¹/₄ teaspoon salt
¹/₂ cup lite mayonnaise
¹/₄ cucumber, peeled and finely chopped
1 clove garlic, minced
¹/₄ teaspoon dried dill weed

1. Spread onion over trout fillets in a microwave-proof dish. Sprinkle with salt. Cover dish tightly with plastic wrap; turn back one corner.
2. Microwave on MEDIUM 5 minutes.
3. Mix mayonnaise, cucumber, garlic, and dill weed. Spread over trout. Microwave on MEDIUM 3 minutes.
4. Let stand 1-2 minutes to complete cooking.

Makes 6 servings
. . . .
Substitutions: Salmon fillets, catfish, mackerel
Calculations per Serving: 206 calories, 10 gm total fat,
   2 gm saturated fat, 69 mg cholesterol, 207 mg sodium
Diabetic Exchanges: 3¹/₂ meat

Italian-Breaded Sea Bass

1 pound sea bass fillets
1 tablespoon margarine, melted
¹/₄ cup Italian bread crumbs
1 tablespoon parsley, chopped
¹/₈ teaspoon black pepper
¹/₈ teaspoon paprika

1. Melt margarine in microwave-proof dish. Add
   sea bass to dish, coating both sides with melted
   margarine.
2. Combine bread crumbs, parsley, and seasonings in a
   small bowl. Sprinkle crumb mixture over sea bass.
3. Cover with paper towel. Microwave on MEDIUM
   5-7 minutes or until fish just flakes when tested with
   a fork. Let stand 1-2 minutes to complete cooking.

Makes 4 servings

Substitutions: Salmon, trout, bluefish
Calculations per Serving: 162 calories, 5 gm total fat,
   1 gm saturated fat, 47 mg cholesterol, 161 mg sodium
Diabetic Exchanges: ¹/₂ bread, 3 meat

Flounder with Dill

1 pound flounder fillets
$^1/_2$ cup low-sodium chicken broth
$^1/_4$ teaspoon black pepper
$^1/_4$ teaspoon dried dill weed
$^1/_4$ teaspoon garlic powder
$^1/_4$ teaspoon salt

1. Place fish fillets in microwave-proof dish.
2. Mix remaining ingredients in a small bowl. Pour over fish.
3. Cover dish with plastic wrap; turn back one corner.
4. Microwave on HIGH 3-6 minutes or until fish just flakes when tested with a fork.
5. Let stand 1-2 minutes to complete cooking.

Makes 4 servings
• • • • • • • • • • • • •

Substitutions: Orange roughy, pollock, bluefish
Calculations per Serving: 136 calories, 2 gm total fat,
  0 gm saturated fat, 77 mg cholesterol, 294 mg sodium
Diabetic Exchanges: 3 meat

South American Cod

¹/₂ pound cod fillets
1 tomato, chopped
¹/₃ cup onion, chopped
¹/₄ cup parsley, chopped
3 tablespoons green chilies, diced
1 tablespoon lime juice
¹/₄ teaspoon dried oregano
¹/₄ teaspoon sugar
¹/₄ teaspoon black pepper
¹/₄ teaspoon salt
Lime wedges
Green pepper strips or sliced green onion

1. Place fish in microwave-proof baking dish.
2. Combine tomato, onion, parsley, chilies, lime juice, oregano, sugar, pepper, and salt in a small bowl.
3. Pour tomato mixture over fish. Cover dish with plastic wrap; turn back one corner.
4. Microwave on HIGH 4-6 minutes or until fish just flakes when tested with a fork.
5. Let stand 1-2 minutes to complete cooking. Garnish with lime wedges, green pepper strips, or green onion as desired.

Makes 2 servings
• • • • • • • • • • • •

Substitutions: Orange roughy, pollock, halibut
Calculations per Serving: 148 calories, 1 gm total fat,
  0 gm saturated fat, 49 mg cholesterol, 336 mg sodium
Diabetic Exchanges: 2 vegetable, 3 meat

Ginger-Sesame Sole Fillets

1 pound sole fillets
2 tablespoons water
2 tablespoons green onion, chopped
1 teaspoon lite soy sauce
1 tablespoon sesame oil
1 clove garlic, minced
2 teaspoons fresh ginger, grated
1/4 teaspoon black pepper
1/2 teaspoon toasted sesame seeds

1. Combine water, green onion, soy sauce, sesame oil, garlic, ginger, and pepper in a small bowl.
2. Arrange fillets in a single layer in microwave-proof dish.
3. Spread ginger mixture over fillets.
4. Cover dish with plastic wrap; turn back one corner. Microwave on HIGH 3-5 minutes or until fish just flakes when tested with fork. Let stand 1-2 minutes to complete cooking.
5. Sprinkle with sesame seeds and serve.

Makes 4 servings
• • • • • • • • • • •
Substitutions: Flounder, cod, pollock
Calculations per Serving: 176 calories, 6 gm total fat,
  1 gm saturated fat, 77 mg cholesterol, 166 mg sodium
Diabetic Exchanges: 3¹/₂ meat

Spicy Orange Roughy

1 pound orange roughy fillets
2 teaspoons curry powder
1 teaspoon onion powder
1 teaspoon ground cumin
$^1/_2$ teaspoon ground ginger
$^1/_2$ teaspoon turmeric
$^1/_2$ teaspoon garlic powder
$^1/_4$ teaspoon salt

1. Mix seasonings together in a bag. Put fish in bag and shake to coat.
2. Arrange fish in shallow microwave-proof dish. Sprinkle with remaining coating. Cover with paper towel.
3. Microwave on HIGH 4-6 minutes or until fish just begins to flake when tested with a fork. Let stand covered 1-2 minutes to complete cooking.

Makes 4 servings

Substitutions: Croaker, haddock, shrimp
Calculations per Serving: 152 calories, 8 gm total fat,
 0 gm saturated fat, 23 mg cholesterol, 207 mg sodium
Diabetic Exchanges: 3$^1/_2$ meat

Tuna Steak with Lemon Pepper

1 pound tuna steak
$^{1}/_{4}$ cup white wine
2 cloves garlic, minced
1 teaspoon olive oil
1 teaspoon lemon pepper seasoning
$^{1}/_{4}$ teaspoon black pepper
$^{1}/_{4}$ teaspoon salt
4 thin slices onion, separated into rings
$^{1}/_{2}$ lemon, thinly sliced

1. Place fish in microwave-proof dish.
2. Combine wine, garlic, olive oil, lemon pepper seasoning, pepper, and salt in a small bowl. Stir. Pour over fish.
3. Marinate in refrigerator 15-20 minutes.
4. Top fish with onion and lemon slices. Cover dish with plastic wrap; turn back one corner. Microwave on HIGH 4-6 minutes or until fish just turns opaque. Let stand 1-2 minutes to complete cooking.

Makes 4 servings
. . . .

Substitutions: Swordfish, salmon, marlin, mahi mahi
Calculations per Serving: 190 calories, 7 gm total fat,
   2 gm saturated fat, 43 mg cholesterol, 333 mg sodium
Diabetic Exchanges: 3 meat

Tomato Salsa Catfish

1 pound catfish fillets
1/3 cup salsa
1/2 teaspoon Worcestershire sauce
1/2 teaspoon vegetable oil
1/4 teaspoon black pepper
1/4 teaspoon salt
1/8 teaspoon paprika

1. Combine salsa with Worcestershire sauce, oil, and seasonings in small bowl. Stir well.
2. Place catfish in microwave-proof dish. Pour salsa mixture over fish.
3. Cover dish with plastic wrap; turn back one corner. Microwave on HIGH 4-6 minutes or until fish just flakes when tested with a fork. Let stand 1-2 minutes to complete cooking.

Makes 4 servings

Substitutions: Orange roughy, sea bass, flounder
Calculations per Serving: 141 calories, 5 gm total fat,
  2 gm saturated fat, 66 mg cholesterol, 356 mg sodium
Diabetic Exchanges: 3 meat

Mexican Shrimp

2 pounds shrimp, peeled and deveined
2 tablespoons olive oil
1 tablespoon lime juice
2 cloves garlic, minced
$1/2$ teaspoon dried red pepper flakes
$1/4$ teaspoon ground cumin
$1/4$ teaspoon black pepper

1. Combine olive oil, lime juice, garlic, and seasonings in microwave-proof dish. Microwave on HIGH 30 seconds.
2. Add shrimp in a single layer.
3. Cover dish with plastic wrap; turn back one corner. Cook on HIGH 2-3 minutes, stirring every minute until shrimp just turns pink.
4. Let stand 1-2 minutes to complete cooking.

Makes 8 servings

Substitutions: Scallops, oysters, crayfish, slippertail lobster
Calculations per Serving: 122 calories, 5 gm total fat,
  1 gm saturated fat, 129 mg cholesterol, 126 mg sodium
Diabetic Exchange: 2 meat

Lemon Parsley Shrimp

1 pound shrimp, peeled and deveined
2 tablespoons margarine
¼ cup white wine or low-sodium chicken broth
2 tablespoons parsley, chopped
2 tablespoons lemon juice
3 cloves garlic, minced
¼ teaspoon lemon pepper seasoning

1. Melt margarine in a microwave-proof dish.
2. Stir in wine, parsley, lemon juice, garlic, and lemon pepper seasoning. Add shrimp. Stir to coat. Cover dish with plastic wrap; turn back one corner.
3. Microwave on HIGH 2-3 minutes, stirring every minute until shrimp just turns pink. Let stand 1-2 minutes to complete cooking.

Makes 4 servings
. . . .
Substitutions: Scallops, halibut, oysters
Calculations per Serving: 155 calories, 7 gm fat,
   1 gm saturated fat, 129 mg cholesterol, 241 mg sodium
Diabetic Exchanges: 3 meat

Oriental Shrimp

1 pound shrimp, peeled and deveined

<u>Sauce</u>

¹/₄ cup green onion, chopped
2 tablespoons water
2 tablespoons rice vinegar
1 tablespoon brown sugar
1 tablespoon lite soy sauce
1 tablespoon sesame oil
1 teaspoon cornstarch
¹/₄ teaspoon black pepper

1. Combine sauce ingredients in microwave-proof dish.
   Microwave on HIGH 1 minute or until thickened.
   Stir once during cooking.
2. Add shrimp to sauce. Microwave on HIGH 2-3
   minutes, stirring every minute until shrimp just turns
   pink. Let stand 1-2 minutes to complete cooking.

Makes 4 servings

Substitutions: Cod fillets, halibut fillets, pollock fillets, scallops
Calculations per Serving: 138 calories, 5 gm total fat,
   1 gm saturated fat, 129 mg cholesterol, 266 mg sodium
Diabetic Exchanges: ¹/₂ fruit, 3 meat

Grilling

11

Grilling

Fresh Tuna with Cilantro

1 pound tuna steaks
Vegetable cooking spray

<u>Marinade</u>
$^1/_2$ cup white wine
$^1/_4$ cup cilantro, finely chopped
1 tablespoon olive oil
1 tablespoon dry mustard
1 tablespoon chili powder
1 teaspoon black pepper
$^1/_4$ teaspoon salt

1. Mix marinade ingredients in a small bowl. Reserve
   2-3 tablespoons marinade for basting.
2. Pour marinade over tuna. Marinate for 15-20 minutes,
   turning once. Spray fish with vegetable cooking spray.
3. Grill tuna over hot coals for 3 minutes. Turn. Brush
   with reserved marinade after turning. Grill 4-5
   minutes longer.

Makes 4 servings
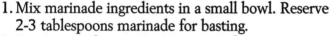

Substitutions: Swordfish, marlin, halibut, cod
Calculations per Serving: 234 calories, 10 gm total fat,
  2 gm saturated fat, 43 mg cholesterol, 201 mg sodium
Diabetic Exchanges: 4 meat

Beer-Basted Salmon

1 pound salmon
1 12-ounce can beer
1 teaspoon dried basil

1. Cover grill with heavy-duty aluminum foil. Fold up one inch of foil along each side to contain beer.
2. Pour beer into foil and bring to a boil over hot coals. Gently place salmon into beer. Baste salmon with beer. Sprinkle with basil.
3. Close the lid of the grill. Grill 10 minutes per inch, basting throughout.

Makes 4 servings

Calculations per Serving: 146 calories, 4 gm total fat, 1 gm saturated fat, 59 mg cholesterol, 78 mg sodium
Diabetic Exchanges: 3 meat

Grilled Whole Salmon

1 whole salmon (about 4 pounds), dressed[1]
¹/₄ teaspoon lemon pepper seasoning
¹/₄ teaspoon dried thyme
¹/₄ teaspoon dried marjoram
¹/₄ teaspoon dried basil
1 lemon, thinly sliced
1 medium onion, thinly sliced
1 cup parsley sprigs
Vegetable cooking spray

1. Rinse fish with cold water. Pat dry.
2. Make three shallow diagonal slashes into each side of the salmon.
3. Sprinkle lemon pepper, thyme, marjoram, and basil inside salmon belly cavity.
4. fill belly with lemon, onion, and parsley sprigs.
5. Spray fish with vegetable oil.
6. Place in oiled, hinged wire basket.[2] Grill over hot coals. Allow 10 minutes per inch of thickness measured at its thickest point.
7. Turn midway through cooking.
8. Ease onto serving platter. Serve plain or with your favorite sauce.

Makes 12-16 servings
. . . .

Substitutions: Whole bluefish, trout
Calculations per Serving: 142 calories, 4 gm total fat,
   1 gm saturated fat, 84 mg cholesterol, 70 mg sodium
Diabetic Exchanges: 4 meat

[1] Dressed fish have been gutted, scaled, headed, and trimmed of their fins.
[2] May be wrapped in foil.

Citrus Grilled Halibut

1 pound halibut fillets or steaks
Vegetable cooking spray

<u>Marinade</u>
¹/₄ cup orange juice
2 tablespoons lite soy sauce
1 tablespoon olive oil
1 tablespoon lemon juice
1 clove garlic, minced
¹/₄ teaspoon black pepper
¹/₄ teaspoon salt

1. Combine marinade ingredients in nonmetallic bowl.
   Reserve 2-3 tablespoons marinade.
2. Pour marinade over halibut. Marinate fish 15-20
   minutes, turning once. Spray fish with vegetable
   cooking spray.
3. Place fish over hot coals. Grill 3 minutes. Turn. Brush
   with reserved marinade. Grill 4-5 minutes.

Makes 4 servings

Substitutions: Salmon, swordfish, tuna
Calculations per Serving: 168 calories, 6 gm total fat,
   1 gm saturated fat, 36 mg cholesterol, 473 mg sodium
Diabetic Exchanges: 3 meat

Zesty Lemon Shark

1¹/₂ pounds shark steaks
Vegetable cooking spray

Marinade
¹/₂ cup lemon juice
2 tablespoons olive oil
2 tablespoons prepared horseradish
1 teaspoon lemon peel, grated
¹/₂ teaspoon salt
¹/₂ teaspoon black pepper
¹/₂ teaspoon dried oregano

1. Place shark in a shallow nonmetallic dish.
2. Blend marinade in a small bowl; set aside 2-3 tablespoons for basting. Pour marinade over fish. Marinate 15-20 minutes, turning once. Coat fish with vegetable cooking spray.
3. Grill 3 minutes over hot coals. Turn. Baste with reserved marinade and grill 4-5 minutes.

Makes 6 servings

Substitutions: Swordfish, tuna, marlin
Calculations per Serving: 172 calories, 7 gm total fat,
 1 gm saturated fat, 57 mg cholesterol, 206 mg sodium
Diabetic Exchanges: 3¹/₂ meat

Hawaiian Tuna

1¹/₂ pounds tuna steaks
Vegetable cooking spray

Marinade
3 tablespoons pineapple juice
¹/₂ teaspoon dry mustard
2 cloves garlic, minced
1 teaspoon brown sugar
1 tablespoon fresh ginger, grated
3 tablespoons lite soy sauce
2 tablespoons dry sherry

1. Combine marinade ingredients in a nonmetallic dish. Reserve 2-3 tablespoons marinade for basting. Add tuna. Marinate 15-20 minutes, turning once.
2. Drain fish from marinade. Coat fish with vegetable cooking spray. Grill over hot coals 3 minutes.
4. Turn. Brush with reserved marinade. Cook an additional 4-5 minutes..

Makes 6 servings

Substitutions: Swordfish, orange roughy, shark
Calculations per Serving: 161 calories, 5 gm total fat,
   1 gm saturated fat, 57 mg cholesterol, 229 mg sodium
Diabetic Exchanges: 3¹/₂ meat

HINT
*Also excellent
broiled in oven.*

Snappy Barbecued Catfish

2 pounds catfish fillets
Vegetable cooking spray

Marinade
1/3 cup lemon juice
1/4 cup green onion, chopped
2 tablespoons ketchup
2 tablespoons olive oil
2 cloves garlic, minced
2 teaspoons sugar
2 teaspoons Worcestershire sauce
1/4 teaspoon cayenne pepper
1/4 teaspoon black pepper

1. Combine marinade ingredients in a shallow non-metallic dish. Reserve 2-3 tablespoons for basting.
2. Add catfish and turn fillets to coat evenly. Marinate 15-20 minutes, turning once.
3. Drain fish. Coat fish with vegetable cooking spray.
4. Grill 3 minutes. Turn. Baste with reserved marinade. Cook 4-5 minutes.

Makes 8 servings

Substitutions: Salmon, halibut, haddock
Calculations per Serving: 177 calories, 8 gm total fat, 2 gm saturated fat, 65 mg cholesterol, 121 mg sodium
Diabetic Exchanges: 3 meat

HINT
Excellent when broiled in oven.

Orange Roughy California with Salsa

1 pound orange roughy
Vegetable cooking spray

Salsa
2 medium Roma tomatoes, coarsely chopped
1/4 cup red onion, chopped
1/4 cup cilantro, chopped
3 tablespoons green chilies, diced
1/4 teaspoon salt
2-3 drops hot pepper sauce (Tabasco)
Marinade
1/3 cup lime juice
1/4 cup beer or low-sodium chicken broth
3 cloves garlic, minced
2 tablespoons cilantro, chopped
1 tablespoon olive oil
1/2 teaspoon ground cumin
1/4 teaspoon black pepper
1/4 teaspoon salt

1. Mix salsa ingredients in a small bowl. Chill until needed.
2. Combine marinade ingredients in a shallow non-metallic dish. Reserve 2-3 tablespoons.
3. Add orange roughy and marinate 15 minutes, turning once.
4. Drain orange roughy. Coat fish with vegetable cooking spray. Grill 4-5 inches over hot coals 3 minutes.
5. Brush with reserved marinade. Turn. Brush again with reserved marinade. Cook an additional 3-4 minutes or until fish flakes when tested with a fork. Top with salsa.

Makes 4 servings
• • • • • • • • • • • •
Substitutions: Halibut, cod, flounder
Calculations per Serving: 136 calories, 4 gm total fat,
   0 gm saturated fat, 23 mg cholesterol, 292 mg sodium
Diabetic Exchanges: 1 vegetable, 3 meat

Jamaican Swordfish

1 pound swordfish steaks
Vegetable cooking spray

<u>Jamaican Rub</u>
2 tablespoons dried minced garlic
2 tablespoons ground ginger
1 teaspooon ground allspice
1 teaspooon ground cloves
1 tablespoon ground cinnamon
1 teaspooon salt
$^1/_8$ teaspooon cayenne pepper
Vegetable cooking spray

1. Mix rub ingredients until blended. Cover tightly until ready to use.
2. Rub 1 tablespoon of seasoning blend on both sides of swordfish.
3. Spray swordfish with vegetable cooking spray.
4. Grill fish over hot coals 3 minutes. Turn. Grill 4-5 minutes.

Makes 4 servings .
• • • • • • • • • • • •
   Substitutions: Halibut, shark, orange roughy
   Calculations per Serving: 144 calories, 5 gm total fat,
     1 gm saturated fat, 44 mg cholesterol, 403 mg sodium
   Diabetic Exchanges: 3 meat

HINT
Store extra rub in an airtight container. Use 1 tablespoon per pound of seafood.

Roasted Oysters in the Shell

Oysters in shell - 12 large, 20 medium, or 32 small

1. Scrub oyster shells thoroughly.
2. Place oysters on a barbecue grill about 4 inches from hot coals, cup-side* resting on the grill. Barbecue until shells begin to open, approximately 5-10 minutes. (The larger the oyster, the longer the cooking time.) Baste with water or beer.
3. Continue cooking 4-6 minutes.

Makes 4 servings
• • • • • • • • • • •

Calculations per Serving: 57 calories, 2 gm total fat, 0 gm saturated fat, 35 mg cholesterol, 74 mg sodium
Diabetic Exchanges: 1 meat

HINT

*Oysters in the shell have two sides. The lid of the oyster is flat. The cup of the oyster is bowl-shaped. In order to retain the juice in the oyster, be sure to place oysters with the cup-side resting on the grill.

Skewered Shrimp

1 pound large shrimp, peeled and deveined
Vegetable cooking spray

<u>Basting sauce</u>
2 tablespoons margarine, melted
2 tablespoons parsley, chopped
1 tablespoon lemon juice
$^1/_4$ teaspoon paprika
$^1/_4$ teaspoon garlic powder

1. Skewer shrimp, about 6-8 per skewer.
2. Combine basting sauce ingredients.
3. Brush shrimp with sauce. Spray with vegetable
   cooking spray. Grill over hot coals 3-6 minutes or
   until shrimp turn pink.

Makes 4 servings

Substitutions: Salmon cubes, scallops, swordfish cubes
Calculations per Serving: 143 calories, 7 gm total fat,
    1 gm saturated fat, 129 mg cholesterol, 203 mg sodium
Diabetic Exchanges: 3 meat

HINT
*Add fruits or
vegetables to the
skewers with the
shrimp.*

Grilled Teriyaki Salmon

1 pound salmon steaks or fillets
Vegetable cooking spray

<u>Marinade</u>
$^1/_2$ cup white wine
$^1/_4$ cup brown sugar
3 tablespoons lite soy sauce
4 cloves garlic, minced
$^1/_2$ teaspoon ground ginger or 1 teaspoon fresh
    ginger, grated

1. Combine marinade ingredients in a shallow
   nonmetallic dish. Reserve 2-3 tablespoons marinade.
2. Marinate fish 15-20 minutes, turning once. Drain fish.
3. Coat fillets with vegetable cooking spray.
4. Grill fish over hot coals 3 minutes. Turn. Brush with
   reserved marinade. Grill 4-5 minutes.

Makes 4 servings
• • • • • • • • • • • •
   Substitutions: Bluefish, swordfish, orange roughy
   Calculations per Serving: 180 calories, 4 gm total fat,
    1 gm saturated fat, 84 mg cholesterol, 268 mg sodium
   Diabetic Exchanges: $^1/_2$ fruit, 3 meat

Grilling Guidelines

Fish	Weight or Thickness	Grilling Method	Grill Heat	Doneness Test & Approx. Cooking Time
WHOLE FISH (With or without head & tail)	½-1 lb. (1 to 1½ in.)	Indirect	Hot	flakes when prodded in thickest part; 12 min.
	3-5 lb. (2 to 2½ in.)	Indirect	Hot	flakes when prodded in thickest part; 30-35 min.
	5-7 lb. (3 in.)	Indirect	Hot	flakes when prodded in thickest part; 45 min.
STEAKS, FILLETS	½ in.	Direct	Hot	flakes when prodded in thickest part; 4-6 min.
	¾ in.	Direct	Hot	flakes when prodded in thickest part; 6-8 min
	1 in.	Direct	Hot	flakes when prodded in thickest part; 8-10 min
	1½ in.	Indirect	Hot	flakes when prodded in thickest part; 15-18 min.
BONELESS CUBES	1 in.	Direct	Hot	flakes when prodded in thickest part; 8-10 min.
SHRIMP	Medium size	Direct	Hot	Shrimp turns pink; 5-7 min.
SCALLOPS	About 1 in.	Direct	Hot	Cut to test; opaque at center, 5-7 min.
CLAMS	Medium size in shells	Direct	Hot	Shells pop open; 3-4 min.
OYSTERS	Medium size in shells	Direct	Hot	Shells pop open; 4-6 min.

Special Events

12

Special Events

Oyster Champagne Stew

1 pound shucked extra small oysters
2 cups champagne or low-sodium chicken broth
4 teaspoons Worcestershire sauce
1 tablespoon fresh ginger, grated
2 teaspoons celery salt
1 13-ounce can evaporated skim milk
1 tablespoon parsley, chopped
¹/₄ teaspoon paprika

1. Combine oysters, champagne, Worcestershire sauce, ginger, and celery salt in a medium saucepan. Bring to a boil, reduce heat, and simmer until oysters are firm and edges curl, about 2 minutes.
2. Stir in milk and heat. Do not boil stew after adding milk.
3. Garnish each serving with parsley and paprika.

Makes 6 servings

Calculations per Serving: 141 calories, 2 gm total fat,
 1 gm saturated fat, 44 mg cholesterol, 473 mg sodium
Diabetic Exchanges: 1 milk

Entertaining with a flair

Bread Bowls: Slice off tops of small round sourdough bread loaves. Hollow out loaves, leaving ¹/₂ inch of bread around outside of bread bowl. Ladle hot stew or chowder into bread bowl and serve. Cut hollowed-out bread into 1-inch cubes. Toast if desired to make croutons for serving with the stew or chowder.

Sunday Dinner

Halibut Pot Roast

Our family used to have a big dinner on Sunday—sometimes it was midday, sometimes in the evening, but always something to look forward to. The eating was good: Dungeness crab, fresh picked oysters, razor clams, or smoked salmon were our usual fare, along with whatever was canned, pickled, or frozen from our huge garden.

The dinners were an ending and a beginning to a week of school and work. Our family sat and chatted for an hour or more. Our Sunday dinners set us up for the days ahead and took the sting out of some of the activities of days past.

Set aside one day, whatever day is convenient, once in a while for a family meal. Start with a Halibut Pot Roast.

Halibut Pot Roast

2-pound halibut roast
8 carrots, peeled and cut in half
8 red potatoes, whole
8 celery stalks, cut in half
1 cup water
1 teaspoon chicken-flavored bouillon granules
3 cloves garlic, minced
$^1/_2$ teaspoon dried dill weed
$^1/_4$ teaspoon black pepper
$^1/_2$ cup parsley, chopped

1. Put fish in center of a large baking pan. Arrange vegetables around fish.
2. Combine water, bouillon, garlic, dill weed, and pepper in a microwave-proof dish. Microwave on HIGH 3 minutes to dissolve bouillon. Stir to mix. Pour over fish and vegetables.
3. Cover pan with lid or foil.
4. Bake at 400° F. 45 minutes.
5. Transfer fish and vegetables to heated serving dish. Garnish with parsley.
6. Drizzle pan drippings over top.

Makes 8 servings

Substitution: Salmon roast
Calculations per Serving: 261 calories, 3 gm total fat,
  0 gm saturated fat, 36 mg cholesterol, 187 mg sodium
Diabetic Exchanges: 2 bread, 3 meat

Old-Fashioned Thanksgiving Salmon

1 whole salmon (about 4-6 pounds[1]), dressed
1 teaspoon dried sage
$^3/_4$ teaspoon black pepper
$^1/_2$ teaspoon salt
2 cups water
Oyster stuffing (See next page)

1. Cut two pieces of foil larger than the size of fish.
2. Place salmon on a piece of foil in roasting pan.
3. Mix sage, pepper, and salt.
4. Rub seasonings inside cavity of salmon.
5. Spoon oyster stuffing inside salmon. Cover salmon with second piece of foil and crimp edges to seal.
6. Pour water in bottom of roasting pan
7. Cover and bake at 325° F. 1 to 1$^1/_2$ hours.

[1]Can use two boneless fillets by layering stuffing between the fillets.

Oyster Stuffing

1 10-ounce jar oysters
2 tablespoons margarine
1 cup low-sodium chicken broth
1 cup parsley, finely chopped
¹/₂ cup onion, minced
¹/₂ cup celery, minced
¹/₂ cup green bell pepper, minced
2 cloves garlic, minced
¹/₄ teaspoon black pepper
¹/₄ teaspoon salt
4 cups toasted bread cubes

1. Drain oysters. Reserve liquid. Chop oysters into small pieces.
2. Melt margarine in frying pan. Add chicken broth, parsley, onion, celery, bell pepper, garlic, black pepper, and salt. Sauté until tender.
3. Mix vegetables, oysters, and bread cubes in large bowl. Moisten stuffing as needed with oyster liquid.
4. Stuff salmon. (See previous page.)

Makes 10 servings
· · · · · · · · · · ·

Substitutions: Shrimp, crab
    2 gm saturated fat, 104 mg cholesterol, 398 mg sodium
Calculations per Serving: 281 calories, 9 gm total fat,
    2 gm saturated fat, 104 mg cholesterol, 398 mg sodium
Diabetic Exchanges: ¹/₂ bread, 4 meat

Easter Buffet Crab Quiche

1 pound crab meat
1 onion, chopped
1 tablespoon margarine
6 whole eggs
12 egg whites
$^1/_2$ cup flour
1 tablespoon Old Bay seasoning
1 teaspoon baking powder
$^1/_4$ teaspoon salt
1 pound nonfat cottage cheese
1 pound lowfat mozzarella cheese, grated

1. Microwave onion in margarine on HIGH 2 minutes.
2. Beat whole eggs and egg whites in large bowl. Add onions, flour, Old Bay seasoning, baking powder, and salt. Mix well. Add crab and cheeses. Stir.
3. Pour into a 9 x 13 inch baking dish. Bake at 450° F. 15 minutes. Reduce oven to 350° F. and bake 30 minutes.
4. Allow quiche to sit 10 minutes before serving.

Makes 15 servings

Substitutions: Imitation crab, shrimp meat
Calculations per Serving: 200 calories, 8 gm total fat,
   5 gm saturated fat, 123 mg cholesterol, 522 mg sodium
Diabetic Exchanges: $^1/_2$ bread, 3 meat

HINT

Using egg whites in place of whole eggs helps reduce the cholesterol values for this recipe.

Poor Man's Lobster

2 pounds halibut, cut into 3-inch long fingers
2 quarts water
2 large onions, sliced thinly
1 carrot, sliced
1 tablespoon sugar
1/4 cup apple cider vinegar
2 bay leaves
1 teaspoon salt

1. Bring water to boil in a large pot. Add onions, carrot, sugar, vinegar, bay leaves, and salt. Boil 5 minutes.
2. Add halibut. Return to boil; turn heat down to medium, and cook 10 minutes. Do not stir.
3. Remove fish. Serve with Rich-in-flavor Sauce (below).

<u>Rich-in-flavor Sauce</u>
1/4 cup lemon juice
1 tablespoon margarine
1 tablespoon olive oil
2 cloves garlic, minced
1/4 teaspoon dried thyme
1/4 teaspoon paprika
1/4 teaspoon black pepper
1/4 teaspoon salt

1. Place all ingredients in a small saucepan.
2. Heat to melt margarine and blend flavors.
3. Pour over halibut.

Makes 8 servings
. . . .

Calculations per Serving: 184 calories, 6 gm total fat,
    1 gm saturated fat, 36 mg cholesterol, 246 mg sodium
Diabetic Exchanges: 1/2 bread, 3 meat

Clam Linguine

1 pound clam meat, minced
6 Roma tomatoes, chopped
¹/₄ cup pine nuts
2 tablespoons parsley, chopped
2 tablespoons lemon juice
2 teaspoons dried basil
2 cloves garlic, minced
¹/₂ teaspoon salt
¹/₄ teaspoon lemon pepper seasoning
1 pound fresh linguine or 8 ounces dried linguine
¹/₄ cup Parmesan cheese, grated

1. Combine clam meat, tomatoes, pine nuts, parsley, lemon juice, basil, garlic, salt, and lemon pepper in a saucepan. Bring to a boil.
2. Reduce heat and simmer uncovered 15-20 minutes. Stir occasionally.
3. Cook pasta according to package directions and drain.
4. Return pasta to kettle and toss with about half of the sauce. Divide among 6 deep plates.
5. Top with remaining sauce. Sprinkle with Parmesan cheese. Serve at once.

Makes 6 servings

Substitutions: Chopped squid, cooked shrimp meat
Calculations per Serving: 258 calories, 5 gm total fat,
   1 gm saturated fat, 28 mg cholesterol, 268 mg sodium
Diabetic Exchanges: 2 bread, 1 meat

HINT

Substitute your favorite pasta for linguine. You can also substitute 8 ounces of dry pasta for one pound fresh pasta.

Focaccia Sandwich

1 15³/₄-ounce can pink salmon, drained and
  skin removed
1 large focaccia bread, split in half lengthwise
¹/₂ cup salsa
¹/₂ cup lite mayonnaise
1 avocado, chopped
1 tomato, thinly sliced
¹/₂ cup white onion, thinly sliced
2 cups alfalfa sprouts
6 slices fatfree Swiss cheese

1. Lay each half of split focaccia bread, cut-side up on
   cutting board.
2. Mix salmon, salsa, and mayonnaise in a bowl. Spread
   over top half of bread.
3. Layer remaining ingredients on bottom half of bread.
4. Place bread halves together. Slice into 8 wedges.

Makes 8 servings
· · · · · · · · · · · ·

> **Substitutions:** Shredded romaine lettuce can be substituted for
> alfalfa sprouts. Use any sandwich fillings with focaccia bread.
> **Calculations per Serving:** 244 calories, 11 gm total fat,
>   2 gm saturated fat, 18 mg cholesterol, 517 mg sodium
> **Diabetic Exchanges:** 1¹/₂ bread, 2 meat, 1 fat

Seafood Puff Shells

1 cup water
¹/₂ cup margarine
1 cup flour
¹/₄ teaspoon salt
¹/₈ teaspoon ground cayenne
1 whole egg
2 egg whites

1. Combine water and margarine in a saucepan and bring to a boil.
2. Add flour all at once and stir vigorously until mixture forms a ball and leaves the sides of the pan. Remove from heat. Cool 5 minutes.
3. Add whole egg and egg whites, one at a time, beating vigorously by hand after each addition. Continue beating until a stiff dough is formed.
4. Drop by tablespoon on a cookie sheet. Bake at 425° F. 15 minutes. Reduce heat to 350° F. and continue baking about 10 minutes until golden brown.
5. Cool before filling.

Makes 20 servings
• • • • • • • • • • •

Smoked Salmon filling
1 7³/₄-ounce can smoke-flavored salmon, drained and flaked
¹/₂ cup lettuce, finely chopped
2 tablespoons lite mayonnaise
2 tablespoons parsley, chopped
2 tablespoons bacon bits

1. Combine salmon with remaining ingredients in medium-sized bowl. Mix.
2. Cut off tops of puff shells. fill each shell.
3. Serve immediately.

Lobster filling
1 cup lobster meat, diced finely
¹/₂ cup tomato, diced
2 tablespoons green onion, minced
2 tablespoons celery, finely minced
2 tablespoons lite mayonnaise
¹/₄ teaspoon lemon pepper seasoning

1. Combine lobster with remaining ingredients in medium-sized bowl. Mix.
2. Cut off tops of puff shells. fill each shell.
3. Serve immediately.

> **Substitutions:** Canned tuna, crab, imitation crab
> **Calculations per Serving:** 26 calories, 2 gm total fat,
>   0 gm saturated fat, 5 mg cholesterol, 43 mg sodium
> **Diabetic Exchanges:** 3 servings are free

Recreational Fishing

13

Recreational Fishing

Concerns for the Recreational or Subsistence Angler

State and local agencies monitor the safety of waters used for recreational fishing. Fishing is forbidden in waters that are considered contaminated. State and local actions protect individuals consuming sport caught seafood by:

- Posting advisories to warn anglers when there is a potential for poisoning or illness
- Warning individuals to limit intake of a certain species to a specific number of servings per week.

To be safe...

- Call the local health department to check the status of fishing waters
- Heed warnings posted on public beaches!

Potential Concerns for Sport-Caught Seafood	
Type of Illness	Greatest Concern
Bacteria	• Fecal bacteria • *Vibrio* family, especially *V. Vulnificus*
Viruses	• Norwalk Virus • Hepatitis A
Parasites	• Roundworm (*Anisakis simplex*)
Naturally-occurring poisons	• Ciguatera • Paralytic Shellfish Poisoning • Scombroid Poisoning
Environmental contaminants	• Mercury • Polychlorinated Biphenyls (PCBs)

Bacterial and Viral Infection

If disease organisms are present in growing waters, shellfish will filter them from the water and retain them. These pathogens may not harm the shellfish but may cause illness in humans.

Source	Raw contaminated shellfish.
	Common bacteria: Fecal Bacteria, Vibrio Family
	Common viruses: Norwalk Virus, Hepatitis A
Location	Seafood harvested from contaminated water.
Potential Severity	Mild to serious
Symptoms	Gastroenteritis
	Symptoms usually resolve in 24-28 hours. If diarrhea and vomiting persist, a physician should be consulted.
Special Considerations	Typically destroyed by thorough cooking.
Safety Steps	The FDA requires that each container of shellfish must be tagged to indicate the source of the shellfish. (Tags trace the shellfish to a specific area and a particular harvester.)

- Avoid consuming raw shellfish.
- Ask to see tags.
  Badly contaminated growing areas are restricted from shellfish harvesting. In areas of less contamination, harvesters may be required to purify shellfish before shipping, The shellfish is kept in holding tanks for several days. This process is called depuration.
- For extra safety, steam mussels, clams, and oysters for 4-6 minutes after the shells are opened.
- Buy shellfish from reputable sources. Check tags and labels at your seafood counter. Avoid taking advantage of a good bargain at a roadside stand. You might get more than you bargained for!
- If you feel that you've become ill from eating raw or undercooked shellfish, contact your local health department and the FDA.

Concerns for Medically "High Risk" Individuals

Vibrio Vulnificus is a naturally-occurring organism which is found in the bacterial flora found in warm, coastal waters. It is a naturally occurring bacteria and not the result of pollution. Therefore, *vibrio may be present* in approved shellfish harvesting waters.

Vibrio Vulnificus does not pose a threat to healthy consumers. However, some individuals in a medically "high risk" category can develop a severe, potentially fatal, blood poisoning.

Source	Bacteria
Location	Warm coastal states
Species Affected	*Raw* Molluscan shellfish, primarily oysters
Potential Severity	• Potentially fatal blood poisoning to "high risk" individuals
	• Insignificant threat to healthy consumers
Symptoms	Blood poisoning
Consumers at High Risk	Individuals with:
	• AIDS
	• Liver disease, including cirrhosis and hemochromatosis
	• Cancer (especially during chemotherapy and radiation treatment)
	• Chronic alcohol use
	• Lymphoma, leukemia, Hodgkins disease
	• Diabetes mellitus
	• Chronic kidney disease
	• Achlorydria (a condition which reduces normal stomach acidity)
	Also at risk:
	• Those taking immunosuppressive drugs
	• Persons taking drugs that reduce normal stomach acidity
Special Considerations	• Reports of illness are most prevalent during the warm months of the year, primarily April through October.
	• Thorough cooking destroys the *vibrio* bacteria. Molluscan shellfish must be steamed 4-6 minutes after water returns to a boil for the internal temperature to rise sufficiently to destroy *Vibrio Vulnificus*.

**Concerns for Medically
"High Risk" Individuals, continued**

- Individuals at risk must also be careful to protect open wounds from seawater or the liquid from raw shellfish.

Safety Steps | "High risk" consumers **must avoid eating all raw shellfish.**

Parasitic Infection

Sushi has become a national passion with sushi bars in most metropolitan areas and individual portions available in many grocery store delicatessans. Some raw seafood may contain parasites that can cause illness. However, according to the Center for Disease Control, parasite infections from fish are rare in this country.

Source	The parasite *Anisakis Simplex.* Worldwide, there are three types of parasitic infections: tapeworms, flukes, and roundworms. The roundworm, *Anisakis s.*, is the only parasite of significance in US seafood.
Location	The Atlantic and Pacific Coasts
Species Affected	*Raw* or *improperly cooked* herring, salmon, and Pacific rockfish fillets. More commonly found in the posteriod body cavity.
Potential Severity	Mild to moderate
Symptoms	• In some cases, the worm is ingested and passed out of the body without producing any symptoms.
	• The roundworm can attach to the stomach and intestinal lining, causing intense pain, nausea, and vomiting.
	• In severe cases, surgical removal of the attached roundworm may be necessary.
Special Considerations	• Parasites are a problem only when fish are consumed raw or undercooked. Raw fish products include sushi, sashimi, ceviche, fish roe, and "green herring."
	• Parasites are destroyed if seafood is frozen at -4° F. for 72 hours. Most home freezers do not reach this temperature.
	• Cold smoking, salting, or marinating will not kill *Anisakis s.*
	• Heating to an internal temperature of 140° F. for 5 minutes will kill parasites.

Safety Steps

- Proper cooking and freezing will destroy all active parasites and result in a completely safe product.
- Purchase raw fish products from a reputable restaurant or manufacturer.

Naturally-Occurring Poisons

Ciguatera

Ciguatera is a natural toxin found in fish that feed on tropical reefs. Eighty percent of all cases of ciguatera are caused by recreational fishing in high-risk areas.

Primary Source	Toxin
Location	The Caribbean and Pacific Islands
	A few outbreaks reported in southern Florida.
Species Affected	Large predatory fish, namely amberjack, barracuda, tropical snappers and tropical groupers
Potential Severity	Mild to temporarily debilitating
Symptoms	Immediate (3-5 hours after ingestion):
	• Abdominal pain, diarrhea, nausea, vomiting
	• Short duration
	Long-term symptoms (12-18 hours after ingestion):
	• Muscular aches
	• Tingling and numbness of lips, tongue, and mouth area
	• Metallic taste in mouth
	• Confusion of hot - cold sensations
	• Dizziness
	• Blurred vision
	Long-term symptoms may be moderate to severe. May persist for several months in severe cases.
Special Considerations	• There is no visual evidence of ciguatera poisoning.
	• The toxin cannot be destroyed by heat.
Safety Steps	• Become familiar with local species which pose potential risk when fishing in tropical waters.
	• ***Heed official warnings!!!!***

Paralytic Shellfish Poisoning

Paralytic Shellfish Poisoning (PSP) is one of the best known and most potent seafood toxins. Approximately 80% of PSP cases result from harvesting shellfish *in closed coastal areas*. Shellfish feed on toxic plankton, become toxic, and remain toxic for several weeks after the plankton bloom subsides.

Source	Toxin
	Commonly known as "red tide"
Location	Coastal states
Species Affected	Molluscan shellfish, namely clams, oysters, mussels, and scallops
Potential Severity	• Potentially life-threatening • Among the most potent toxins known
Symptoms	Normally occur within one hour of ingestion: • Tingling, numbness, and/or burning of mouth, lips, face, neck, and extremities • Lack of coordination • Drowsiness, incoherence • Difficulty with speech • Rash • Fever In severe cases, respiratory paralysis can cause death.
Special Considerations	• The presence of the toxin cannot be detected except by laboratory analysis. • The toxin cannot be destroyed by cooking. • Toxic blooms occur most frequently during warmer months, most frequently between April and October.
Safety Steps	• Coastal states carefully monitor the presence of PSP and close *all* shellfish harvesting in affected areas. • Call the health department for harvesting status. • Heed warnings posted on public beaches.

Scombroid Poisoning

Scombroid poisoning results from eating fish which have been improperly handled or stored. If fish is not quickly and properly chilled after capture, bacteria on the surface will convert the aminoacid histidine to histamine and can cause an allergic response.

Source	Histamine poisoning (spoiled fish)
Location	Widespread, but more prevalent in warm climates
Species Affected	Primarily mahi mahi, tuna, and bluefish. Less often: amberjack, anchovies, herring, jack, mackerel, and sardines
Potential Severity	Mild to moderate *continued*
Symptoms	May appear within a few minutes to four hours after consuming toxic fish: • Flushing of the face and possibly upper body; may resemble sunburn • Tingling and burning of the mouth and/or throat • Mouth dryness/difficulty swallowing • Fever, sweating • Severe throbbing headache • Heart palpitations • Abdominal pain, nausea, vomiting, diarrhea • Rash, hives, itching • Muscular pain, weakness, dizziness Symptoms usually last 8-12 hours and respond well to antihistamines.
Special Considerations	• Neither cooking nor freezing will destroy toxin once present in fish. • Fish may not have a foul odor. • Histamine may produce a "metallic" or "peppery" taste when eaten.
Safety Steps	• Recreational fishermen should gut, bleed, and *immediately* chill potentially toxic fish. • Proper handling of (recreationally-caught) seafood is the only way to prevent Scombroid poisoning. • FDA monitors the histamine levels in canned tuna and fresh/frozen fish. • Buy fish only from a reputable dealer. • Immediately refrigerate your seafood after purchase. Store in the coldest part of your refrigerator (between 32-38° F.).

Environmental Contaminants

Mercury

Mercury is a naturally-occurring metallic substance. Minute quantities of mercury are present in air, water, soil, and all living matter. Mercury exists in many forms. Methylmercury is the most toxic to humans. The major problem with mercury has been caused by uncontrolled dumping of industrial waste into inland waters. Industrial discharges are now regulated by state and federal agencies.

Source — Industrial Pollution

Location — Freshwater lakes, rivers, creeks, and reservoir

Species Affected — Large, predatory fish, most commonly swordfish and tuna, Molluscan shellfish, oysters, clams, and mussels.

Potential Severity — The average consumer faces very little risk of methyl-mercury consumption from commercial sources of swordfish and tuna. Commercial fishermen capture swordfish and tuna at sea, far from any potential industrial pollution.
Mercury can be transferred to the fetus via the placenta and can accumulate in the brain and kidney. In children exposed to *excessive* levels of mercury during pregnancy and breastfeeding, mental retardation can occur. Women of childbearing age should limit their consumption of recreationally-caught fish containing 1.0 ppm mercury to 8 ounces per month.
• Methylmercury poisoning can affect the central nervous system in rare cases associated with excessive intakes of recreationally-captured seafood. The FDA carefully monitors commercially-harvested swordfish and tuna.

Safety Steps — The FDA's current limit for mercury is 1 part per million (1 ppm). When levels exceed 1 ppm, advisories are issued to commercial and recreational fishermen.
Heed consumption advisories!!!!

Polychlorinated Biphenyls (PCBs)

Polychlorinated biphenyls include more than 200 different compounds once widely used in a variety of industrial products such as electrical equipment, carbonless copy paper, plastics, and hydraulic fluids. Although PCBs have been banned for almost twenty years, they remain in the environment because they are very slow to decompose.

Source	Industrial pollution
Location	The Great Lakes, Hudson River, Boston Harbor, and coastal urban harbors
Species Affected	Large, fatty freshwater fish such as salmon, lake trout, carp, and catfish. PCBs accumulate in the internal organs and fatty tissues. *continued*
Potential Severity	• The average consumer faces very little risk of exposure if eating a wide variety of *commercially-harvested* seafood from many different areas.
	• PCBs are considered potential carcinogens.
	• Possible neurological damage to offspring of mothers consuming high levels of PCB-contaminated fish from *recreational sources*.
	• Highly susceptible groups: Women of childbearing age Pregnant women Nursing women and their nursing children
Special Considerations	• PCBs are heat-resistent.
	• A single exposure to PCB-contaminated food is relatively harmless; the threat occurs with repeated consumption and the accumulation of PCBs in the body.
Safety Steps	• The FDA's current limit for PCB levels in the edible part of fish is 2 parts per million (2 ppm). When levels exceed 2 ppm, advisories are issued to commercial and recreational fishermen. ***Heed consumption advisories!***
	• Recent studies suggest that 50% of the PCBs in fish can be reduced through proper preparation and cooking techniques. See the box on the following page.

Tips for Reducing Your Potential Intake of PCBs

- Eat a variety of fish and shellfish.
- Heed consumption advisories.
- Choose smaller fish; they are less likely to contain contaminants.
- Remove skins.
- Avoid eating internal organs.
- Use cooking methods that allow fats to drip away from the flesh (grilling, broiling, baking on a rack).
- Discard all cooking liquids.
- Avoid coatings and breadings that hold in fats and oils.

Selected Bibliography

Bang, H.O., Dyerberg, J., Sinclair, H.M. "The composition of the Eskimo food in northwestern Greenland." *American Journal of Clinical Nutrition.* 1980; 33: 2657-2661.

Childs, M.T., Dorsett, C.S., Failor, A., Roidt, L., Omenn, G.S. "Effect of shellfish consumption on cholesterol absorption in normolipidemic men." *Metabolism.* 1987; 36: 31-36.

Childs, M.T., Dorsett, C.S., King, I.B., Ostrander, J.G., Yamanaka, W.K. "Effects of shellfish consumption of lipoproteins in normolipidemic men." *American Journal of Clinical Nutrition. 1990;* 51: 1020-1027.

Food and Nutritional Board, Institute of Medicine. *Seafood Safety.* Committee on Evaluation on the Safety of Fishery Products. Ahmed F.E., Editor. Washington, DC: National Academy of Sciences, 1991.

Kromhout, D., Bosschieter E.B., and de Lezanne Coulander C. "The inverse relation between fish consumption and 20-year mortality from coronary heart disease." *New England Journal of Medicine.* 1985; 312: 1205-1209.

Leaf, A. Cardiovascular effects of fish oils—beyond the platelet. *Circulation.* 1990; 82: 624-628.

Leaf A., Jorgenson M.B., Jacobs, A.K., et al. Do fish oils prevent testnosis after coronary angioplasty? *Circulation.* 1994; 90: 2248-2257.

Nettleton, J.A. "Are n-3 fatty acids essential nutrients for fetal and infant development?" *Journal of the American Dietetic Association.* 1993; 93: 58-64.

Nutrition Monitoring Division, Human Nutrition Information Service. *Composition of Foods: Finfish and Shellfish Products.* Washington, DC: US Department of Agriculture, Handbook 8-15.

Siscovick, D.S. "Dietary intake and cell membrane levels of long-chain n-3 polyunsaturated fatty acids and the risk of primary cardiac arrest." *Journal of the American Medical Association.* 1995; 274: 1363-1367.

Index by Title

10-Minute-Per-Inch Rule for Fish, 48

A

Alaska Salmonburgers, 88
All Shapes and Sizes, 43
Appetizers, 57
Are Omega-3 Fatty Acids Essential for Good Health?, 14

B

Bacterial and Viral Infection, 212
Baked Parmesan Salmon Loaf, 125
Baked Seafood Linguine, 160
Bayou Barbecued Catfish, 134
Beer-Basted Salmon, 182
Blue Plate Special Halibut, 122
Bourbon Street Gumbo, 76
Breaded Oysters Parmesan, 158
Broiled Catfish with Herb Sauce, 115
Broiled Sesame Scallops, 152
"Butterfly Cut" Shrimp, 144

C

Cajun Baked Flounder, 117
Captain's Night Seafood Stew, 78
Caribbean Haddock, 166
Chinese Seafood Salad, 102
Ciguatera, 215
Citrus Grilled Halibut, 184

Clam Diggers Dip, 64
Clam Linguine, 204
Classic Shrimp and Pea Salad, 112
Cod Veracruz, 164
Concerns for Medically "High Risk" Individuals, 213
Concerns for Sulfite-Sensitive Individuals, 31
Concerns for the Recreational or Subsistence Angler, 211
Consider Safety First...Avoid Eating Raw Seafood, 25
Consider Safety First...Buy From a Reputable Source, 23
Consider Safety First...When Handling Seafood in Your Home, 28
Crab Fettuccine, 145
Crab Louie, 101
Crab Quesadillas, 97
Creamed Salmon over Noodles, 136
Crispy Cod, 120
Curry Seafood Stew with Lentils, 77

D

Diabetes, 11
Dry Heat Cooking Techniques, 51

E

Easter Buffet Crab Quiche, 202
Elegant Scallops, 153

Environmental Contaminants, 218

F

Facts About Seafood Safety, 1
Family Favorite Tuna Noodle Casserole, 126
Finfish Entrées, 113
Flounder with Dill, 169
Focaccia Sandwich, 205
Fresh Tuna with Cilantro, 181

G

Garden Fresh Coleslaw with Shrimp, 107
Ginger Crab Salad, 105
Ginger Sesame Shrimp, 142
Ginger-Sesame Sole Fillets, 171
Grilled Swordfish Caesar Salad, 109
Grilled Teriyaki Salmon, 192
Grilled Whole Salmon, 183
Grilling, 179
Grilling Guidelines, 193

H

Halibut Pot Roast, 199
Halibut Stirfry, 127
Halibut Vegetable Chowder, 84
Hawaiian Tuna, 186
Health Food from the Sea, 3
Herb-Stuffed Oysters, 66
Historical Perspective, 8

Hot Crab and Artichokes, 69
How Safe is Seafood?, 21
How to Clean a Mussel, 45
How to Clean a Shrimp, 46
How to Cook Heart Smart, 48
How to Crack a Crab, 46
How to Dress a Lobster, 47
How to Dress a Soft-Shell Crab, 46
How to Dress a Squid, 47
How to Evaluate a Seafood Counter, 35
How to Fillet a Flat Fish, 44
How to Fillet a Round-Bodied Fish, 44
How to Open a Clam, 45
How to Pick Out the Best and Keep it That Way, 36
How to Shuck an Oyster, 45
How to Steak a Salmon, 44
How to Substitute Seafood, 39

I

If You Are the Source of Your Seafood..., 24
Is Shellfish Heart-Healthy?, 15
Island Fresh Cucumber Salad, 111
Italian-Breaded Sea Bass, 168
Italian-Crumbed Orange Roughy, 131

J

Jamaican Swordfish, 189

K

Keeping Seafood Safe at Home, 40

L

Landing a Seafood Bargain, 55
Lemon Parsley Shrimp, 176
Lobster Beach Bake, 147
Louisiana Catfish, 137

M

Majority of Seafood Illness..., 22
Manhattan Seafood Chowder, 79
Marinated Ginger Tuna, 123
Marinated Jumbo Shrimp, 60
Maryland Crab Cakes, 89
Maui Shrimp Burrito, 95
Mercury, 218
Mexican Cod, 121
Mexican Crab Dip, 68
Mexican Fiesta Salad, 104
Mexican Seafood Soup, 80
Mexican Shrimp, 175
Microwave, 161
Moist Heat Cooking Techniques, 49

N

Neptunes, 61
New England Clam Chowder, 81
Nutrition, 1
Nutritional Comparisons, 17

O

Ocean Perch Dijon, 124
Old-Fashioned Thanksgiving Salmon, 200
Omega 3's and Cancer, 10
Omega-3's and Heart Disease, 9
One-Dish Halibut, 165
Open-Faced Crab Muffins, 91
Orange Roughy California with Salsa, 188
Oriental Shrimp, 177
Oriental Stirfry, 132
Other Health Benefits, 13
Oyster Champagne Stew, 197
Oyster Sauté, 157
Oyster Stuffing, 201

P

Paralytic Shellfish Poisoning, 216
Parasitic Infection, 214
Poached Salmon, 130
Polychlorinated Biphenyls (PCBs), 219
Poor Man's Lobster, 203
Preparation, 33

Q

Quick Steamed Snapper, 129

R

Raw Finfish, 26
Raw Shellfish, 25
Ready to Eat Processed Seafood, 53
Recreational Fishing, 209

Refreezing
Seafood, 42
Roasted Oysters in
the Shell, 190

S

Safety, 19
Salads, 99
Salmon and
Garbanzo Pita
Bread, 92
Salmon
Cheese Ball, 71
Salmon
Florentine, 163
Salmon Melt
Supreme, 90
Salmon
Nuggets, 138
Salmon
Pinwheels, 70
Salsa Baked Oysters
in the Shell, 159
San Francisco
Cioppino, 83
Sandwiches, 85
Sardine
Sandwich, 96
Saturday Night
Pizza, 87
Scallops
Almandine, 154
Scombroid
Poisoning, 217
Seafood
Puff Shells, 206
Seafood
Taco Soup, 82
Seaside Shells, 65
Seviche-Style
Surimi, 110
Shellfish
Entrées, 139
Shrimp and Broccoli
Salad, 103
Shrimp and Tomato
Pasta, 141

Shrimp and Tomato
Tostada, 93
Shrimp Corn
Chowder, 75
Shrimp Feast in
Beer, 143
Shrimp Taco with
Corn Salsa, 94
Shrimp-Cashew
Fruit Salad, 106
Shrimp-Spinach
Salad with Orange
Dressing, 108
Shrimp-Stuffed
Celery, 59
Skewered
Scallops in Peanut
Sauce, 62
Skewered
Shrimp, 191
Smoked Seafood, 53
Smoky Salmon Pâté
with Toasted
Bagels, 63
Snappy Barbecued
Catfish, 187
Soups and Stews, 73
Sources of
Additional Safety
Information, 32
South American
Cod, 170
Southwest Style
Catfish, 119
Special Events, 195
Spicy Orange
Roughy, 172
Spicy Pecan Crunch
Haddock, 118
Spicy Steamed
Mussels, 156
Squid Sauté, 150
Steamed Clams, 155
Steamed Mussels in
Beer, 67

Stuffed Italian Squid
Manicotti, 146
Sulfites, 31
Summertime Crab
Enchiladas, 151
Sunday Dinner, 198

T

Tarragon Pollock
Sauté, 135
Thawing Frozen
Seafood, 42
Tips for Reducing
Your Potential
Intake of
PCBs, 220
Tomato Salsa
Catfish, 174
Trout with Cucum-
ber Sauce, 167
Trout with Green
Chili and Orange
Salsa, 116
Tuna Melt, 98
Tuna Steak with
Lemon Pepper, 173

U

Unique Benefits of
Seafood, 7

V

Vibrio
Vulnificus, 213

W

Whole Live
Lobster, 148
Why Seafood
Twice a Week?, 5
Wine Poached
Sole, 128

Z

Zesty Lemon
Shark, 185

Index

This index is intended to be used as a cross reference. Entries are listed under categories and by types of fish that may be substituted in any given recipe.

For example, under **SHRIMP** there is an appetizer recipe for **Shrimp Stuffed Celery**. This recipe also appears under **CRAB** as crabmeat is one of the possible seafood substitutions for that recipe.

ALL SHAPES AND SIZES, 43

BACTERIA
Vibrio Vulnificus, 25, 213
BASS
Entrées
Bayou Barbecued Catfish, 134
BENEFITS OF SEAFOOD, 3, 7, 13, 15
BLUEfiSH
Entrées
Flounder with Dill, 169
Italian-Breaded Sea Bass, 168
Poached Salmon, 130
Salmon Florentine, 163
Southwest Style Catfish, 119
Trout with Green Chili and Orange Salsa, 116
Grilling
Grilled Teriyaki Salmon, 192
Grilled Whole Salmon, 183

CATFISH
Entrées
Bayou Barbecued Catfish, 134
Broiled Catfish with Herb Sauce, 115
Cajun Baked Flounder, 117
Louisiana Catfish, 137
Poached Salmon, 130
Southwest Style Catfish, 119
Tomato Salsa Catfish, 174
Trout with Cucumber Sauce, 167
Grilling
Snappy Barbecued Catfish, 187
Soups and Stews
Halibut Vegetable Chowder, 84
CLAMS
Appetizers
Clam Diggers Dip, 64
Herb-Stuffed Oysters, 66
Steamed Mussels in Beer, 67
Entrées
Clam Linguine, 204
Crab Fettuccine, 145
Shrimp Feast in Beer, 143
Spicy Steamed Mussels, 156

Steamed Clams, 155
How to Open, 45
Soups and Stews
Captain's Night Seafood Stew, 78
New England Clam Chowder, 81
San Francisco Cioppino, 83
COCKLES
Entrées
Spicy Steamed Mussels, 156
Steamed Clams, 155
COD
Entrées
Blue Plate Special Halibut, 122
Caribbean Haddock, 166
Cod Veracruz, 164
Crispy Cod, 120
Ginger-Sesame Sole Fillets, 171
Italian-Crumbed Orange Roughy, 131
Mexican Cod, 121
Oriental Shrimp, 177
Poached Salmon, 130
Quick Steamed Snapper, 129
South American Cod, 170

COD, continued
Southwest Style
Catfish, 119
Tarragon Pollock
Sauté, 135
Trout with Green
Chili and Orange
Salsa, 116
Grilling
Fresh Tuna with
Cilantro, 181
Orange Roughy
California with
Salsa, 188
Soups and Stews
Manhattan Seafood
Chowder, 79
San Francisco
Cioppino, 83
Seafood
Taco Soup, 82
**CONCERNS
FOR SULFITE
SENSITIVE
INDIVIDUALS, 31**
**COOKING
TECHNIQUES**
Dry Heat, 51, 52
Moist Heat, 49, 50
CRAB
Appetizers
Clam Diggers
Dip, 64
Hot Crab and
Artichokes, 69
Mexican
Crab Dip, 68
Shrimp-Stuffed
Celery, 59
Entrées
Baked Seafood
Linguine, 160
Crab
Fettuccine, 145
Easter Buffet Crab
Quiche, 202
Seafood Puff
Shells, 206
Summertime Crab
Enchiladas, 151
How to Crack, 46
How to Dress, 46

Salads
Classic Shrimp and
Pea Salad, 112
Crab Louie, 101
Garden Fresh
Coleslaw with
Shrimp, 107
Ginger
Crab Salad, 105
Mexican Fiesta
Salad, 104
Shrimp-Cashew
Fruit Salad, 106
Shrimp-Spinach
Salad with Orange
Dressing, 108
Sandwiches
Crab
Quesadillas, 97
Maryland Crab
Cakes, 89
Shrimp and Tomato
Tostada, 93
Shrimp Taco with
Corn Salsa, 94
Tuna Melt, 98
Side Dishes
Oyster
Stuffing, 201
Soups and Stews
Bourbon Street
Gumbo, 76
Captain's Night
Seafood Stew, 78
Mexican Seafood
Soup, 80
San Francisco
Cioppino, 83
Seafood
Taco Soup, 82
CRAB, IMITATION
Appetizers
Mexican
Crab Dip, 68
Seaside Shells, 65
Shrimp-Stuffed
Celery, 59
Entrées
Easter Buffet Crab
Quiche, 202
Seafood Puff
Shells, 206

Summertime Crab
Enchiladas, 151
Salads
Chinese Seafood
Salad, 102
Classic Shrimp and
Pea Salad, 112
Crab Louie, 101
Seviche-Style
Surimi, 110
Shrimp and
Broccoli
Salad, 103
Sandwiches
Maryland Crab
Cakes, 89
Open-Faced Crab
Muffins, 91
Salmon and
Garbanzo Pita
Bread, 92
Salmon Melt
Supreme, 90
Saturday Night
Pizza, 87
Soups and Stews
Seafood
Taco Soup, 82
CRAWFISH
Entrées
Shrimp Feast in
Beer, 143
CRAYFISH
Entrées
Mexican
Shrimp, 175
CROAKER
Entrées
Spicy Orange
Roughy, 172

**DISEASE
PREVENTION,
5, 13**
Diabetes, 11
**DISEASE, RISK OF,
21, 22**
Bacterial and Viral
Infection, 212
Ciguatera, 215

Concerns for
Medically
"High Risk"
Individuals, 213
Paralytic Shellfish
Poisoning, 216
Parasitic
Infection, 214
Raw Finfish, 26
Raw Shellfish, 25
Recreational
Fishing, 209
Scombroid
Poisoning, 217
Vibrio Vulnificus,
25, 213

ENVIRONMENTAL
CONTAMINANTS,
218
Concerns for the
Recreational or
Subsistence
Angler, 211
Mercury, 218
Polychlorinated
Biphynels
(PCBs), 219

FLAT FISH
How to Fillet, 44
FLOUNDER
Entrées
Bayou Barbecued
Catfish, 134
Cajun Baked
Flounder, 117
Crispy Cod, 120
Flounder
with Dill, 169
Ginger-Sesame
Sole Fillets, 171
One-Dish
Halibut, 165
Tarragon Pollock
Sauté, 135
Tomato Salsa
Catfish, 174
Wine Poached
Sole, 128

Grilling
Orange Roughy
California with
Salsa, 188
Soups & Stews
San Francisco
Cioppino, 83

GRILLING
GUIDELINES, 193
GROUPER
Entrées
Broiled Catfish
with Herb
Sauce, 115
Salmon
Nuggets, 138

HADDOCK
Entrées
Caribbean
Haddock, 166
Italian-Crumbed
Orange
Roughy, 131
Spicy Orange
Roughy, 172
Spicy Pecan Crunch
Haddock, 118
Grilling
Snappy Barbecued
Catfish, 187
HALIBUT
Entrées
Blue Plate Special
Halibut, 122
Broiled Sesame
Scallops, 152
"Butterfly Cut"
Shrimp, 144
Caribbean
Haddock, 166
Elegant
Scallops, 153
Halibut
Pot Roast, 199
Halibut Stirfry, 127
Lemon Parsley
Shrimp, 176
Mexican Cod, 121

One-Dish
Halibut, 165
Oriental
Shrimp, 177
Oriental
Stirfry, 132
Poor Man's
Lobster, 203
Salmon
Nuggets, 138
South American
Cod, 170
Squid Sauté, 150
Grilling
Citrus Grilled
Halibut, 184
Fresh Tuna with
Cilantro, 181
Jamaican
Swordfish, 189
Orange Roughy
California with
Salsa, 188
Snappy Barbecued
Catfish, 187
Salads
Grilled Swordfish
Caesar Salad, 109
Soups and Stews
Halibut Vegetable
Chowder, 84
New England Clam
Chowder, 81
San Francisco
Cioppino, 83
HOW TO . . .
Clean a Mussel, 45
Clean a Shrimp, 46
Crack a Crab, 46
Dress a Lobster, 47
Dress a Soft-Shell
Crab, 46
Dress a Squid, 47
Fillet a Flat Fish, 44
Fillet a Round-
Bodied Fish, 44
Open a Clam, 45
Shuck an Oyster, 45
Steak a Salmon, 44

LING COD
Entrées
Cajun Baked
Flounder, 117
Marinated Ginger
Tuna, 123
Soups and Stews
Halibut Vegetable
Chowder, 84
LOBSTER
Appetizers
Mexican
Crab Dip, 68
Entrées
"Butterfly Cut"
Shrimp, 144
Lobster Beach
Bake, 147
Mexican
Shrimp, 175
Whole Live
Lobster, 148
How to Dress, 47
Salads
Island Fresh
Cucumber
Salad, 111
Mexican Fiesta
Salad, 104
Seviche-Style
Surimi, 110
Shrimp-Cashew
Fruit Salad, 106
Soups & Stews
New England Clam
Chowder, 81

MACKEREL
Entrées
Trout with
Cucumber
Sauce, 167
Trout with Green
Chili & Orange
Salsa, 116
MAHI MAHI
Entrées
Broiled Catfish
with Herb
Sauce, 115
Oriental
Stirfry, 132

Tuna Steak
with Lemon
Pepper, 173
MARLIN
Entrées
Ocean Perch
Dijon, 124
Tuna Steak
with Lemon
Pepper, 173
Grilling
Fresh Tuna with
Cilantro, 181
Zesty Lemon
Shark, 185
MONKfiSH
Entrées
Elegant
Scallops, 153
Halibut Stirfry, 127
Squid Sauté, 150
MUSSELS
Appetizers
Herb-Stuffed
Oysters, 66
Entrées
Shrimp Feast in
Beer, 143
Spicy Steamed
Mussels, 156
How to Clean, 45

NUTRITION, 1
Comparisons, 17

**OMEGA-3 FATTY
ACIDS, 4, 7, 8, 9,
10, 13, 14, 15**
ORANGE ROUGHY
Entrées
Bayou Barbecued
Catfish, 134
Caribbean
Haddock, 166
Cod Veracruz, 164
Flounder with
Dill, 169
Italian-Crumbed
Orange
Roughy, 131
One-Dish
Halibut, 165

Quick Steamed
Snapper, 129
Salmon
Florentine, 163
South American
Cod, 170
Spicy Orange
Roughy, 172
Spicy Pecan Crunch
Haddock, 118
Tomato Salsa
Catfish, 174
Grilling
Grilled Teriyaki
Salmon, 192
Hawaiian
Tuna, 186
Jamaican
Swordfish, 189
Orange Roughy
California with
Salsa, 188
OYSTERS
Appetizers
Herb-Stuffed
Oysters, 66
Steamed Mussels
in Beer, 67
Entrées
Breaded Oysters
Parmesan, 158
Lemon Parsley
Shrimp, 176
Mexican
Shrimp, 175
Oyster Sauté, 157
Salsa Baked
Oysters in the
Shell, 159
Scallops
Almandine, 154
Grilling
Roasted Oysters in
the Shell, 190
How to Shuck, 45
Side Dishes
Oyster
Stuffing, 201
Soups and Stews
Oyster Champagne
Stew, 197

PERCH
Entrées
Crispy Cod, 120
Ocean Perch
Dijon, 124
Salmon
Florentine, 163
Southwest Style
Catfish, 119
POACHED
SALMON, 130
POLLOCK
Entrées
Flounder
with Dill, 169
Ginger-Sesame
Sole Fillets, 171
Oriental
Shrimp, 177
Quick Steamed
Snapper, 129
South American
Cod, 170
Spicy Pecan Crunch
Haddock, 118
Tarragon Pollock
Sauté, 135
Wine Poached
Sole, 128
Soups and Stews
San Francisco
Cioppino, 83
PREPARATION OF
SEAFOOD, 35
10-Minute-Per-Inch
Rule, 48
Thawing Frozen
Seafood, 42
PROCESSED
SEAFOOD, 53

RAW FINFISH
Sushi, Sashimi,
Ceviche, 26
RAW SHELLFISH, 25
RECREATIONAL
FISHING, 209

RISK OF
DISEASE. *SEE*
SAFETY IN
SEAFOOD
Concerns for the
Recreational or
Subsistence
Angler, 211
ROCKFISH
Entrées
Crispy Cod, 120

SABLEFISH
Entrées
Trout with Green
Chili & Orange
Salsa, 116
SAFETY IN
SEAFOOD
Recreational
Fishing, 209
SAFETY PRE-
CAUTIONS, 23, 25,
28, 32, 213, 214,
215, 216, 217, 218,
219, 220
Consider Safety
First...Avoid
Eating Raw
Seafood, 25
Consider Safety
First...Buy From
a Reputable
Source, 23
Consider Safety
First...When
Handling Seafood
in Your Home, 28
How Safe is
Seafood?, 21
If You Are the
Source of Your
Seafood..., 24
Keeping Seafood
Safe at Home, 40
Sources for
Additional Safety
Information, 32

SALMON
Appetizers
Seaside Shells, 65

Smoky Salmon
Pâté with Toasted
Bagels, 63
Entrées
Blue Plate Special
Halibut, 122
Halibut
Pot Roast, 199
Halibut Stirfry, 127
Italian-Breaded
Sea Bass, 168
Old-Fashioned
Thanksgiving
Salmon, 200
One-Dish
Halibut, 165
Poached
Salmon, 130
Salmon
Florentine, 163
Salmon
Nuggets, 138
Spicy Pecan Crunch
Haddock, 118
Tarragon Pollock
Sauté, 135
Trout with
Cucumber
Sauce, 167
Tuna Steak
with Lemon
Pepper, 173
Grilling
Beer-Basted
Salmon, 182
Citrus Grilled
Halibut, 184
Grilled Teriyaki
Salmon, 192
Grilled Whole
Salmon, 183
Skewered
Shrimp, 191
Snappy Barbecued
Catfish, 187
How to Steak, 44
Salads
Ginger
Crab Salad, 105
Grilled Swordfish
Caesar Salad, 109

SALMON, continued
Soups and Stews
Halibut Vegetable
Chowder, 84
New England Clam
Chowder, 81
SALMON, CANNED
Appetizers
Clam Diggers
Dip, 64
Salmon Cheese
Ball, 71
Salmon
Pinwheels, 70
Shrimp-Stuffed
Celery, 59
Entrées
Baked Parmesan
Salmon Loaf, 125
Creamed Salmon
over Noodles, 136
Family Favorite
Tuna Noodle
Casserole, 126
Seafood Puff
Shells, 206
Salads
Chinese Seafood
Salad, 102
Crab Louie, 101
Mexican Fiesta
Salad, 104
Seviche-Style
Surimi, 110
Shrimp and Broccoli
Salad, 103
Shrimp-Cashew
Fruit Salad, 106
Shrimp-Spinach
Salad with
Orange Dressing,
108
Sandwiches
Alaska Salmon-
burgers, 88
Focaccia
Sandwich, 205
Open-Faced Crab
Muffins, 91
Salmon and
Garbanzo Pita
Bread, 92

Salmon Melt
Supreme, 90
Saturday Night
Pizza, 87
Shrimp and Tomato
Tostada, 93
Shrimp Taco with
Corn Salsa, 94
Tuna Melt, 98
SALMON, SMOKED
Appetizers
Salmon
Pinwheels, 70
SARDINES
Sandwiches
Salmon and
Garbanzo Pita
Bread, 92
Sardine
Sandwich, 96
SCALLOPS
Appetizers
Skewered Scallops
in Peanut
Sauce, 62
Entrées
Breaded Oysters
Parmesan, 158
Broiled Sesame
Scallops, 152
"Butterfly Cut"
Shrimp, 144
Crab
Fettuccine, 145
Elegant
Scallops, 153
Ginger Sesame
Shrimp, 142
Lemon Parsley
Shrimp, 176
Mexican
Shrimp, 175
Oriental
Shrimp, 177
Oyster Sauté, 157
Salmon
Nuggets, 138
Scallops
Almandine, 154
Squid Sauté, 150
Steamed
Clams, 155

Grilling
Skewered
Shrimp, 191
Salads
Grilled Swordfish
Caesar Salad, 109
Island Fresh
Cucumber
Salad, 111
Soups and Stews
Captain's Night
Seafood Stew, 78
New England Clam
Chowder, 81
San Francisco
Cioppino, 83
SEA BASS
Entrées
Italian-Breaded
Sea Bass, 168
Tomato Salsa
Catfish, 174
SEAFOOD
BARGAINS, 55
SELECTION OF
SEAFOOD, 36
SHARK
Entrées
Marinated Ginger
Tuna, 123
Ocean Perch
Dijon, 124
Grilling
Hawaiian
Tuna, 186
Jamaican
Swordfish, 189
Zesty Lemon
Shark, 185
Salads
Grilled Swordfish
Caesar Salad, 109
SHRIMP
Appetizers
Clam Diggers
Dip, 64
Marinated Jumbo
Shrimp, 60
Mexican
Crab Dip, 68
Neptunes, 61
Salmon
Pinwheels, 70

Seaside Shells, 65
Shrimp-Stuffed
Celery, 59
Steamed Mussels
in Beer, 67
Entrées
Broiled Sesame
Scallops, 152
"Butterfly Cut"
Shrimp, 144
Clam
Linguine, 204
Crab
Fettuccine, 145
Easter Buffet Crab
Quiche, 202
Elegant
Scallops, 153
Ginger Sesame
Shrimp, 142
Halibut Stirfry, 127
Lemon Parsley
Shrimp, 176
Mexican
Shrimp, 175
Oriental
Shrimp, 177
Oriental
Stirfry, 132
Oyster Sauté, 157
Scallops
Almandine, 154
Shrimp and Tomato
Pasta, 141
Shrimp Feast in
Beer, 143
Spicy Orange
Roughy, 172
Summertime Crab
Enchiladas, 151
Grilling
Skewered
Shrimp, 191
How to Clean, 46
Salads
Chinese Seafood
Salad, 102
Classic Shrimp and
Pea Salad, 112
Crab Louie, 101
Garden Fresh
Coleslaw with
Shrimp, 107

Ginger
Crab Salad, 105
Island Fresh
Cucumber
Salad, 111
Mexican Fiesta
Salad, 104
Seviche-Style
Surimi, 110
Shrimp and Broccoli
Salad, 103
Shrimp-Cashew
Fruit Salad, 106
Shrimp-Spinach
Salad with Orange
Dressing, 108
Sandwiches
Crab
Quesadillas, 97
Maui Shrimp
Burrito, 95
Open-Faced Crab
Muffins, 91
Salmon and
Garbanzo Pita
Bread, 92
Saturday Night
Pizza, 87
Shrimp and Tomato
Tostada, 93
Shrimp Taco with
Corn Salsa, 94
Side Dishes
Oyster
Stuffing, 201
Soups & Stews
Bourbon Street
Gumbo, 76
Captain's Night
Seafood Stew, 78
Curry Seafood
Stew with
Lentils, 77
Mexican Seafood
Soup, 80
Seafood Taco
Soup, 82
Shrimp Corn
Chowder, 75
SMOKED
SEAFOOD, 53

SNAPPER
Entrées
Broiled Catfish
with Herb
Sauce, 115
Italian-Crumbed
Orange
Roughy, 131
Quick Steamed
Snapper, 129
SOLE
Entrées
Ginger-Sesame
Sole Fillets, 171
Wine Poached
Sole, 128
SQUID
Entrées
Clam
Linguine, 204
Oriental
Stirfry, 132
Squid Sauté, 150
Stuffed Italian Squid
Manicotti, 146
How To Dress, 47
STORING
SEAFOOD, 41
Refreezing, 42
STURGEON
Entrées
Marinated Ginger
Tuna, 123
SUBSTITUTING
SEAFOOD, 39
SULfiTES, 31
SWORDFISH
Entrées
Blue Plate Special
Halibut, 122
Mexican Cod, 121
Ocean Perch
Dijon, 124
Tuna Steak
with Lemon
Pepper, 173
Grilling
Citrus Grilled
Halibut, 184
Fresh Tuna with
Cilantro, 181

**SWORDFISH,
continued**
Grilled Teriyaki
Salmon, 192
Hawaiian
Tuna, 186
Jamaican
Swordfish, 189
Skewered
Shrimp, 191
Zesty Lemon
Shark, 185
Salads
Grilled Swordfish
Caesar Salad, 109

TROUT
Entrées
Italian-Breaded Sea
Bass, 168
Salmon
Florentine, 163
Spicy Pecan Crunch
Haddock, 118
Trout with
Cucumber
Sauce, 167
Trout with Green
Chili and Orange
Salsa, 116
Grilling
Grilled Whole
Salmon, 183

TUNA
Entrées
Marinated Ginger
Tuna, 123
Tuna Steak
with Lemon
Pepper, 173
Grilling
Citrus Grilled
Halibut, 184
Fresh Tuna with
Cilantro, 181
Hawaiian
Tuna, 186
Zesty Lemon
Shark, 185
Salads
Grilled Swordfish
Caesar Salad, 109
Mexican Fiesta
Salad, 104
Sandwiches
Salmon Melt
Supreme, 90
Shrimp and Tomato
Tostada, 93
TUNA, CANNED
Appetizers
Seaside Shells, 65
Entrées
Baked Parmesan
Salmon Loaf, 125

Creamed
Salmon over
Noodles, 136
Family Favorite
Tuna Noodle
Casserole, 126
Seafood Puff
Shells, 206
Salads
Chinese Seafood
Salad, 102
Ginger
Crab Salad, 105
Island Fresh
Cucumber
Salad, 111
Shrimp and Broccoli
Salad, 103
Shrimp-Cashew
Fruit Salad, 106
Shrimp-Spinach
Salad with Orange
Dressing, 108
Sandwiches
Alaska Salmon-
burgers, 88
Open-Faced Crab
Muffins, 91
Salmon and
Garbanzo Pita
Bread, 92
Tuna Melt, 98

Ordering Information

Please send me _____ copies of
                    Seafood Twice A Week $14.95 ea _____

Also available:
Please send me _____ copies of
Seafood: A Collection of Heart-Healthy Recipes   13.95 ea _____

Please send me _____ copies of
                    Lighthearted Seafood   10.95 ea _____

Washington residents add sales tax:
                    Seafood Twice A Week   1.22 ea _____

Seafood: A Collection of Heart-Healthy Recipes   1.13 ea _____

                    Lighthearted Seafood   .89 ea _____

Shipping and Handling: 1st book   3.00   _____

                            additional books   1.50 ea _____

                            Total Enclosed $ _____

I've enclosed: ☐ Check   ☐ Money Order

Bill my: ☐ Visa   ☐ Mastercard

Card#_____ Expires _____

Phone: _____

Ship to:
Name _____

Address _____

City _____ State_____ Zip _____

Mail payment to:
   National Seafood Educators
   P.O. Box 60006
   Richmond Beach, WA 98160
   Phone: (206) 546-6410
   FAX: (206) 546-6411

SEAFOOD
TWICE A WEEK

Seafood Twice A Week
ISBN 0-9616426-4-5
Seafood: A collection of Heart-Healthy Recipes-
ISBN 0-9616426-2-9
Lighthearted Seafood
ISBN 0-9616426-1-0

Ordering Information

Please send me ____ copies of
Seafood Twice A Week $14.95 ea   _____

Also available:

Please send me ____ copies of
Seafood: A Collection of Heart-Healthy Recipes   13.95 ea   _____

Please send me ____ copies of
Lighthearted Seafood   10.95 ea   _____

Washington residents add sales tax:
Seafood Twice A Week   1.22 ea   _____

Seafood: A Collection of Heart-Healthy Recipes   1.13 ea   _____

Lighthearted Seafood   .89 ea   _____

Shipping and Handling: 1st book   3.00   _____

additional books   1.50 ea   _____

Total Enclosed $ _____

I've enclosed: ☐ Check   ☐ Money Order

Bill my: ☐ Visa   ☐ Mastercard

Card#_____   Expires _____

Phone: _____

Ship to:
Name _____

Address _____

City _____ State_____ Zip _____

Mail payment to:
National Seafood Educators
P.O. Box 60006
Richmond Beach, WA 98160
Phone: (206) 546-6410
FAX: (206) 546-6411

SEAFOOD
TWICE A WEEK

Seafood Twice A Week
ISBN 0-9616426-4-5
Seafood: A collection of Heart-Healthy Recipes-
ISBN 0-9616426-2-9
Lighthearted Seafood
ISBN 0-9616426-1-0